GOD'S LAWS
OF SUCCESS

GOD'S LAWS
OF SUCCESS

By
Robert Tilton

HARRISON HOUSE
Tulsa, Oklahoma

Third Printing

God's Laws of Success
ISBN 0-89274-405-7
(Formerly ISBN 0-914307-04-05)
Copyright © 1983, 1986 by Robert Tilton
P. O. Box 819000
Dallas, Texas 75381

Published by Harrison House, Inc.
P. O. Box 35035
Tulsa, Oklahoma 74153

Contents

1
THOUGHTS ON SUCCESS

A body of believers usually cannot live and act above the level of the teaching it is receiving. So this teaching on success, happiness, and peace of mind is designed to raise the level of Christian living of those readers who have not had this kind of truth revealed to them previously and to help stabilize or reinforce the teachings for those to whom these truths are familiar.

If people are taught that sometimes God heals and sometimes He does not, then some will get healed and some will not. If people are taught that prosperity is not scriptural, they are not going to have the financial success that could be attained under the premise that prosperity is God's will for them. Those who have been taught that being poor is "meek and humble" and scripturally correct need the revelation in this book as retraining. They need to have their minds reprogrammed according to the Word of God.

Whether these principles are read as a review of previous material or constitute reprogramming of totally new information, the result will mean great things happening in the lives of the readers. My wife, Marte, and I want this book to be a blessing to every reader.

Our church in Dallas, Word of Faith World Outreach Center, didn't happen by accident. We didn't cross our fingers or rub a rabbit's foot and hope. That kind of superstition doesn't work. Our success came through continually applying the principles of God found in His Word. God's principles operating in our lives, we have found, are like the constant dropping of water on a rock. It is not the big splash that grinds the rock down. It is the constant dropping of water on that rock that wears it away.

Continually applying God's principles of success in one's life will bring a Christian into a position of success. It does not happen overnight, but it happens. Everything begins with a seed which gets bigger as it matures. The same principle works where success in anything is concerned.

Heavenly Father, I thank You for the anointing that abides upon Your Word. I thank You for the special anointing and the special gift You have placed within my spirit man to effectively communicate to Your people.

I thank You, Father God, that the blood of the Lord Jesus Christ cleanses us from all unrighteousness. I thank You that we are able to stand in Your presence without fear, inferiority, or guilt.

I thank You, Father God, that Jesus Christ is Lord of this group of readers, and those with whom they deal. We seek to put the Kingdom of God in first place.

I thank You, Father God, that these readers are strong. They are springing up to maturity. They are not influenced by false teaching, nor the elements of this world. They are influenced by Your Spirit and by the doctrines of the Holy Spirit that have been delivered to us. The Spirit of Truth will lead and guide us into all truth.

Through the authority of the name of Jesus, we pray. Amen.

The theme of this book is God's Laws of Success — happiness and peace of mind. God's laws, not man's laws, are involved in these teachings; not doctrines and traditions of men, but the principles of God as revealed in His Word. In order to attain financial freedom and live above the beggarly elements of this world in these last days, we must understand how to operate through

God's words, God's rules and regulations, and God's principles or ways of causing things to happen.

In this series of teachings, we are going to be quite thorough. We will analyze some areas which are possibly new fields of study for some readers. These teachings will help in many areas of life. Some of them are as follows:

Eliminate frustrations in your life.

Release the Holy Spirit in your life.

Change your destiny.

Increase your creativity.

Learn how to deal wisely in all the affairs of life.

Accomplish your goals.

Fulfill the call of God in your life.

Be more productive.

Enjoy more achievement and satisfaction.

Attain financial freedom.

Achieve personal success.

Bring harmony into your ideas, feelings, and actions — in agreement with the will of God.

Be charged with the Life of God.

Have more contentment and pleasure.

Enjoy divine health.

Inherit your inheritance and possess your possessions.

The Spirit of God spoke this to me as I prepared these teachings: *"Jesus came to deliver man from failure and to cause him to be once again a success."* So I believe the teachings in this book constitute one of the major themes that God wants taught to the Body of Christ during this decade. Jesus has been sent by God to deliver humanity from its sins and from death, but also to deliver us from "death" in this life through failure. Jesus came to allow us to become successes in all areas of our lives.

After much time spent studying and meditating on God's Word, I have come to this profound, yet simple, conclusion: The Bible is God's Book of Success. The Bible is the greatest success book that has ever been written. Read and study and meditate on God's Word. Then, by applying those truths in our own lives, we can become the success that God designed us to be.

We began our church with zero money. We came to the Dallas area in a small orange four-by-eight-foot rental trailer. We had money enough to rent a house, and that was all. But we applied the Word of God to our lives and in our situations. And we have seen God continually honor His Word and cause it to be productive in our lives.

Our church, at this time, has a gross worth of more than $10 million. It has a continental and world outreach and has become one of the most prominent churches in America with approximately 8,000 members. This tremendous growth did not happen by accident, nor by wanting, wishing, and hoping. The growth has come about because we continually applied God's Word. We did this every day, whether we felt like it or not. We refused to be moved by what we saw or heard in our circumstances. We did not allow ourselves to become discouraged, but kept ourselves encouraged with the Word of God. His Word works.

We share the story of our success with others, not to brag on ourselves, but as an example of what one congregation has done with the Word of God. Our programs and outreach ministries continue to grow and expand. And what we did, anyone can do by applying God's principles of success consistently.

Planted Seeds Bear Fruit

Everything begins with a seed. The seed of God's Word has to be planted in the heart and nourished. Then it will grow and bring forth fruit. To attain total freedom and to live above the circumstances of this world, a Christian must understand how to operate through God's Word. He has certain principles, certain "rules and regulations." When applied properly, they will bring about desired results.

There are Christians who do not believe in divine healing nor prosperity. They do not believe in all of the things involved in Christ's atonement at Calvary. It amazes me that these believers often are the very ones who continually strive to be healthy and to make money. They work hard to attain what was already atoned for them through the shed blood of Jesus Christ — freedom from the curse of the Law. They are trying to attain by their own works what has already been attained through the atonement instead of receiving the blessing that Jesus went to the cross to provide.

Success is not attainment. It is in the atonement. It is not in our works, but in Jesus' works at Calvary. We must realize it is not what we can *do*, but what we can *receive* that brings success and health and prosperity. And we receive by applying faith in our lives toward God. We have to become aware of our free benefits through Jesus, Who purchased them at Calvary and chose to freely give them to us.

We must make ourselves aware of what God has done through Jesus for us. Once we become aware of what is ours, we can simply receive it. Many Christians are not aware of all the things God has done and lack knowledge of what belongs to them as His children. But through the teaching and the understanding given by the Holy Spirit, we can become alerted to what is rightfully ours.

Success means having a favorable outcome to our endeavors. I believe God wants every one of us to have favorable outcomes. We could say success means having things turn out as planned. When you plan something and it turns out that way, that is success. Success means to attain the desired end. It also means to receive the hoped-for results.

According to Hebrews 11:1, **Faith is the substance of things hoped for.** Thoughts are things and the corresponding action of faith will cause those things hoped for to come to pass and become realities in your life. Not succeeding is failure. Failure is falling short of the mark.

The apostle Paul wrote in Philippians 3:14, **I press toward the mark for the prize of the high calling of God in Christ Jesus.** God wants you to hit the mark. He doesn't want you to fall short. It is the desire of the Spirit of God for you not to be bound nor hindered by falling short. I believe God wants to instruct you through this material so that you can continually hit the mark.

I enjoy shooting and am a good shot. I seldom, if ever, go hunting; but, I enjoy target-shooting games. I enjoy aiming at the target and hitting the mark. When I first began shooting, I didn't hit those little tin targets very often. But I began to train and practice and exercise discipline in hitting the target and began to make progress. I practiced knowing when to shoot. Over a period of time, I became a good marksman at the arcade. Well, it works the same way with God's Word, with the game of life, and with the things God has called you to accomplish through understanding His Word.

There is fulfillment in hitting the target. Whether you are shooting 10 metal ducks for a quarter or real elephants in Africa, the reward comes from hitting the mark. The feeling is the same. Everyone likes that little "pitter-pat, pitter-pat" that we get in our hearts when we hit the mark. That is achievement and fulfillment. And it is pleasurable. God delights in the prosperity of His servants. He enjoys our prosperity. He enjoys it when we hit the mark.

I believe that what is past is past. I'm not interested in past failures. My priority is to release you from your past and bring you into success. The Spirit of God is upon me the same way the Spirit of God was upon the Lord Jesus Christ.

> **The Spirit of the Lord is upon me, because he hath anointed me to preach the gospel to the poor; he hath sent me to heal the brokenhearted, to preach deliverance to the captives, and recovering of sight to the blind, to set at liberty them that are bruised,**
>
> **To preach the acceptable year of the Lord** (the year of Jubilee).
>
> **Luke 4:18,19**

Jesus was saying the Spirit of the Lord had anointed Him to preach the gospel to the poor — to those who were lacking and those who had been failures. And He has sent me to heal the brokenhearted or those who have been defeated. He has sent me to preach deliverance to the captives and recovering of sight to the blind. That includes more than those who cannot see physically.

I believe "recovering of sight" also includes those whom God causes through His Word to be able to see or perceive things correctly as God sees things — from the right vantage point. That's the way we want to see things — from the right vantage point. We need recovery of sight.

We are to set at liberty them that are bruised and to preach the acceptable year of the Lord. In other words, we are to deliver man from the penalties of sin and release man from the low estate of failure. We are to bring man into a high estate of success, into heavenly places, enjoying the creativity and fulfillment of God working in and through us. I am so involved with God working in and through me that my whole life is consumed by it. I am enjoying the fulfillment of God living in and through me. And that is not a state of selfishness, either. It is a state of giving. E. W. Kenyon made this statement, "Success is not in how much you can get, but in how much you can give and release to others."

I like that statement. I think it is one of the best statements he ever made. I believe it is the truth, for I have spent some time studying in God's Word just to find out what success is all about. I like success. I like succeeding. In fact, I don't even plan for failure. I always plan, and my plan is for success. Success is not how much you can get. It is how much you give and release to others. The more you give, the more God gives back to you.

He says, "Since you're having such a good time giving, I'm going to give you some more so that you can give again." Giving is God's principle of success. When we really understand that in our minds and in our spirits, we will really enjoy life.

You must have a purpose in life. People without a purpose are the ones wanting to kill themselves, the ones who have no reason for living. Without a vision, the people perish. But Jesus came to earth to give us a reason for living. Once we are born again, there is the fulfillment of Christ growing up inside of us. Despite any circumstances, we now have growing within us the fruit of the Spirit: **love, joy, peace, longsuffering, gentleness, goodness, faith, meekness, temperance** (Gal. 5:22,23). **For me to live is Christ** (Phil. 1:21).

Once we are born again, we are made into disciples or followers of Christ. Over a period of time, we are to become more like Jesus and enjoy His fulfillment. And I don't believe anyone is ever too old to prosper. You have many years of Christian productivity left. If you believe that, you might as well be as productive and fruitful in those years as God wants you to be.

An Old Testament Success Story

I want to share with you a success story from the Word of God. It is just the first of many stories I want to share with you. This particular story is a beautiful example of a man who goes from failure to success. It is related in 1 Chronicles 4:9,10.

And Jabez was more honourable than his brethren: and his mother called his name Jabez, saying, Because I bare him with sorrow.

And Jabez called on the God of Israel, saying, Oh that thou wouldest bless me indeed, and enlarge my coast, and that thine hand might be with me, and that thou wouldest keep me from evil, that it may not grieve me! And God granted him that which he requested.

This scripture seems to contradict itself. First it says that Jabez was more honorable than his brethren; then it says he was born in sorrow. Actually, it means that Jabez held an honorable position in the tribe of Judah. He was a high-ranking member of his tribe. He held a position of honor. Yet he was a failure. You might say that he was a king without a kingdom. He was exercising dominion over nothing, and then the nothing was exercising dominion over him. He was a failure.

But Jabez did something about it. **And Jabez called on the God of Israel** (v. 10). Jabez called to his covenant God of Israel. He began to take the first step. He had some priorities. He began to give God first place in his life.

It is possible to live above the storms of life in these last days. I want you to know something: The strong will get stronger, and he who has shall have more given unto him. But he who thinks he has something, but really doesn't, will have less. It is the survival of the spiritually fittest in these last days. I believe that those operating in the Word are the only ones who will make it. So we need to make the decision to be the ones operating in it.

Jabez was more honorable than his brethren. His mother named him Jabez because she bore him with sorrow. The word *sorrow* means "under the curse."

Jabez was born under the curse of the law, not under the blessing of God. Sorrow is defined as "disappointments, distress caused by loss, grief, sadness, affliction, and misfortune." He must have been a miserable person, having been born under such a curse. I've met people who seemed to have similar lives. No matter what they did, they missed it. They couldn't handle it. They just never succeeded.

God's Word will deliver us from that. It will bring us into the hitting of the mark, into success instead of failure. Jabez was born under the curse. Can you imagine it? Griefs, sorrows, diseases, lack. Born in the curse. Born in failure. But he didn't stay under the curse. He did something about it: he called on God.

And Jabez called on the God of Israel, saying . . . bless me indeed. In other words, he was saying, "Bless the things I put my hand to accomplish. Bless me in my actions. Bless the fruit of my doings. Bless me, Oh God, in the endeavors of life that I set out to accomplish. God, bless me in life. Bless me indeed."

Next, Jabez said, **That thine hand might be with me.** He asked God to be with him. We know Jesus said, **I will never leave thee, nor forsake thee** (Heb. 13:5). We are born of the Spirit of God. Galatians 3:14 says we are redeemed from the curse, that the blessing of Abraham might come upon us. Then Jabez said, **Keep me from evil, that it may not grieve me!** Evil is something that is not morally good; something that brings sorrow, distress, or calamities. Jabez asks that it not grieve him. Jabez gave God priority in his life. He put God first.

It was as if Jabez said to God: "Oh, God, bless the things that I put my hand to accomplish. Bless me in my actions. Bless me in the endeavors of my life. Enlarge my coast. Give me a greater scope. Let me see things in a greater perspective. Increase my eyesight. Let me see things, oh, God, as You see them!" Jabez cried out to God, and God answered him. Jabez chose God. He chose to be a success.

God granted Jabez his petition. He called on God. Jabez wanted his deeds to be blessed, and his perspective to be correct. He wanted God to be with him. And he wanted to be delivered from evil so that he would no longer be grieved by calamities and sorrows. Jabez had to have a correct vantage point in order to see things correctly or from the right perspective.

I want you to realize that you can be just like Jabez. You can choose to be a success. You don't have to fail at anything in this life. You have been redeemed from failure. Isaiah said this:

> He was despised and rejected and forsaken by men, a Man of sorrows and pains, and acquainted with grief and sickness; and as one from Whom men hide their faces He was despised, and we did not appreciate His worth or have any esteem for Him.
>
> Surely He has borne our griefs — sickness, weakness and distress — and carried our sorrows and pain [of punishment]. Yet we ignorantly considered Him stricken, smitten and afflicted by God [as if with leprosy].
>
> But He was wounded for our transgressions, He was bruised for our guilt and iniquities; the chastisement needful to obtain peace and well-being for us was upon Him, and with the stripes that wounded Him we are healed and made whole.
>
> Isaiah 53:3-5 AMP

Jesus carried our sorrow and griefs. Jesus carried all this on His own body at Calvary. These landmark scriptures tell us:

> Christ hath redeemed us from the curse of the law,
> being made a curse for us: for it is written, Cursed
> is every one that hangeth on a tree:
>
> That the blessing of Abraham might come on the Gen-
> tiles through Jesus Christ; that we might receive the
> promise of the Spirit through faith.
>
> And if ye be Christ's, then are ye Abraham's seed, and
> heirs according to the promise.
>
> **Galatians 3:13,14,29**

I want you to realize that you are redeemed from the curse. You are redeemed from failure so that you can have life. You can have life abounding. You can have an abundance of God's life flowing through you. Jesus came so that we could have life, and have it more abundantly. (John 10:10.)

Tapping the Creativity of God

As for me, I get inspired ideas every day. Every day I am so filled with the creativity of God that I just have to sort out the things I want to utilize. I believe it will be that way on through eternity. I have met people who just are non-creative. They are flat and "blah." I don't believe that is God's way for them to be. I believe God's way is for them to be inspired and healthy and creative and happy. God wants us to be successful and happy and to have peace of mind. He wants us to have peace, with Him in our hearts or spirits, and to have peace of mind.

> Take heed what ye hear: with what measure ye mete,
> it shall be measured to you: and unto you that hear
> shall more be given.
>
> For he that hath, to him shall be given: and he that
> hath not, from him shall be taken even that which he
> hath.
>
> **Mark 4:24,25**

You have been given God's Word — His complete rule book for success, happiness, and peace of mind. As you hear what God says in His Word, and apply that Word to your own life, you will receive even more. It is a basic rule of God. The ones who use what they have been given will be given even more to use.

To truly understand success, you must believe that it does not come upon you from the outside. Success begins on the inside, then it manifests itself outwardly. My prayer is that you will receive this teaching through the Spirit of God, that you will "see" it through the eyes of God and not through carnal eyes. Receive it in the Spirit. Some things come from God in ways the natural mind can't receive. They are foolishness to the natural mind. It thinks they are absurd.

If you plan to really operate in the things of the Spirit, you will have to operate through the Word of God. Sometimes faith and confidence are mistaken by people who see carnally. Seen through the natural eye, it appears to be selfish egotism. Have you ever noticed that? Because a person is bold and confident, people say, "He just has a big ego."

That is not always true. If he is operating out of his spirit, then you are seeing his inner man. That happens to be Christ living big within him. The Bible says the righteous are as bold as a lion. Bold faith has nothing to do with ego. It has to do with a re-created spirit being charged with the overcoming life of God. And we have to be overcomers in these last days or the world will mow us down and the devil will walk all over us.

Receive God's Word into your spirit. Get it down into your heart in abundance. When you do, the outward circumstances of your life will change.

Lay not up for yourselves treasures upon earth, where
moth and rust doth corrupt, and where thieves break
through and steal:

But lay up for yourselves treasures in heaven, where
neither moth nor rust doth corrupt, and where thieves
do not break through nor steal:

For where your treasure is, there will your heart be
also.
                                              Matthew 6:19-21

Your "treasures" are the things you are trusting in.
That is where your heart will be. Where have you
placed your confidence? If you are placing your confidence in the riches and finances of the world system,
then you will be continually moved and swayed as the
circumstances in the world move and change. But by
placing your confidence in the things of God and His
Kingdom, you will stand immovable! You will be like
the tree described in Psalm 1: planted firmly by the
river, bringing forth fruit unto God, prospering in
everything you do.

True success comes from having the right perspective on things. To understand this teaching on success,
you must learn to see through the eyes of God, from
His vantage point. That can only come from time spent
in study and meditation on God's Word.

The light of the body is the eye: if therefore thine eye
be single, thy whole body shall be full of light.
                                              Matthew 6:22

The word evil means "something contrary to good,
something violating moral law, harmful, injurious,
disastrous." Evil includes everything that is bad. By seeing only things that are evil — calamities, distresses,
problems, lack, sickness, failure — your whole body
will be full of darkness.

Finding God's Perspective

Let me give you an example from my own life of how you can have the wrong perspective. I operate in the Word of God. I am strong in the Lord. And all of us are growing up in Christ. Right? I'm growing and learning just as you are. When we were constructing our present facility, we were closing the loan for interim financing of approximately $1.25 million. We were acting as our own general contractor.

For us to be able to receive this financing, we had to place a large sum of money into a savings certificate, like a deposit or an escrow. This was in case of overruns or extra costs during construction. This kind of transaction protects the people who loan money. But it tied up much of our operating funds. We couldn't touch them. We still had the money, but we couldn't use it This caused us to have less available money for operating expenses, and I didn't like that. I did it, however, because we wanted the new building.

But I got the wrong perspective on that transaction for a few seconds. We had several bills due. And I allowed my eye to become "evil" for a few moments. I started seeing us not having enough money, instead of seeing us having plenty of money. I made a mistake. I didn't know at first where I was missing it, but it was as if I had walked into a big cloud. Have you ever done this? Surely you have.

For a few moments, I got into a cloud and couldn't quite put my finger on the open door that was allowing me to move into that cloud. So I asked the Spirit of God. James said, **If any of you lack wisdom, let him ask of God** (James 1:5). I wanted to find out where I had missed God.

You might say, "But, Bob, that was obvious."

No, not to me at that time. Sometimes you can't see the forest for the trees, and you need the Spirit of God to show you where you are missing it. He doesn't mind showing you because He wants you to be a success. He doesn't want you to fail.

I should have been looking at our finances this way: "Praise God, we have more than enough to pay the bills!" I should not have been seeing that we didn't have enough to pay them. And when my "eye" stopped becoming evil through looking at the circumstances and started becoming full of light and single-minded, according to God's Word (spiritually minded), it released me from the cloud. And then I was just as happy as a lark.

I was just looking at things wrong. But because I looked at one little area wrong, it caused me to become double-minded and pushed down by worldly circumstances. I shouldn't have been depressed at all. And, actually, I wasn't. I just recognized a weight on me that wasn't right. That can happen to any of us so quickly if our "eye" gets wrong.

So I just praise God that I have learned to operate in the Spirit and receive from God, and that He can talk to me and I can hear Him. I saw that I was missing it, looking at the situation from the wrong reference point. I was looking down when I should have been praising God and looking up. I pray that you can understand this example and learn from it. In Matthew 6:23, Jesus says, **But if thine eye be evil**. If you see the calamities and the bad things happening around you, your whole body will be full of darkness. But if you start seeing the results and success, and who you are in Christ, then your whole body will be full of light. And you will be seeing things from God's perspective. You will see solutions instead of problems.

You don't have to see situations through darkness. I did in that instance, but I soon changed my perspective. I am pressing toward the mark. I miss it now and then just as you do. Pray for me to hit the mark more often! So we are looking now at the right point of perspective.

> But if thine eye be evil, thy whole body shall be full of darkness. If therefore the light (understanding) that is in thee be darkness, how great is that darkness!
>
> No man can serve two masters: for either he will hate the one, and love the other; or else he will hold to the one, and despise the other. Ye cannot serve God and mammon.
>
> Therefore I say unto you, Take no thought for your life, what ye shall eat, or what ye shall drink; nor yet for your body, what ye shall put on. Is not the life more than meat, and the body than raiment?
>
> Therefore take no thought, saying, What shall we eat? or, What shall we drink? or, Wherewithal shall we be clothed?
>
> Matthew 6:23-25,31

Matthew is talking about things the world strives to get. Get, get, get. Heap together. God is saying, "But that is not My principle, nor My way of doing things." If you think that way leads to success, forget it. You will have nothing but problems. Don't take thought, saying what you are going to do, or wear, or eat, or drink, or how you're going to make it. That is not your first priority. Verse 33 gives the first priority in order to be a success and receive the things of which you have need:

**But seek ye first the kingdom of God, and his
righteousness; and all these things shall be added
unto you.**

Matthew 6:33

Where is the Kingdom of God? It's within the born-again believer. **The kingdom of God cometh not with observation** (outward show) (Luke 17:20). The Kingdom of God is within.

What is the Kingdom of God? According to Romans 14:17, it is **righteousness, and peace, and joy in the Holy Ghost.** Think about this. Righteousness simply means that you are in right standing and in harmony with God, and that what belongs to God belongs to you. Seek first the Kingdom of God. Secondly, seek His righteousness. Being in right standing with God opens the door to benefits. What are they? Divine health, prosperity, success. Those are all benefits of being an heir of God and a joint heir with Jesus. If you are an heir of God, you have clout.

So the Kingdom of God is success because of righteousness. It is peace — peace of mind and peace with God. The Kingdom of God is success, peace of mind, and joy. Being in the Kingdom of God means being successful, having peace of mind, and having happiness in your life. That is what the Kingdom of God is in any endeavor of your life.

Some people believe God allows them to be sick so that they can become spiritually strong. Many who believe that are the ones who go to hospitals. Why in the world do they go to the hospital to work against God's plan to make them strong, if they really believe that? That doesn't even make sense. It doesn't fit. And that's why many Christians are confused and don't really know what to believe. Many people believe two or three things that really contradict each other. So their minds are double, not single. And you have to be single-minded, single-purposed upon the things you want to attain and receive through God. You can't be unsettled and indecisive. You must decide what you are going to do. And then you must believe that you receive it. Of course, *it must be in harmony with God's Word*. Then it is believable for you.

If you understand it and it is in harmony with God's Word, then it is believable. And you will only receive things after they become believable to your spirit. If you want to believe God for something that is not believable, forget it! I don't care how much you say it and confess it, if it's not believable, you won't receive it.

Get Your Priorities Right

Those are the principles of the Kingdom of God for success. The first principle is to get your priorities right. Jabez got his priorities right and called on the covenant God of Israel. The first thing he did was to call upon the One Who could cause him to be blessed in his deeds. He called upon the One Who could increase his vision. He called upon the One Who could give him purpose in life.

Many people commit suicide. They think there is no reason for living. They have no purpose. Yet that is the very thing Jesus came to give humanity — a purpose and a reason for life.

Many people say, "I'm saved. I'm saved."

But some folks don't know what they are saved from nor what they have been delivered from nor in what they have been gloriously blessed. But I know, and I'm excited about what I've been delivered from. And I am overwhelmed about what I've been translated into.

I'm just like a farmer. I get excited about our "crops." I get up in the morning, go to the offices, and go by every one of our little fields that are growing. We have the school field that is growing. And I go check it out and see how the Word is working in it and make sure no weeds are in it. I go to the radio field and see how it is growing, and to the television field, and the Bible school field, and the *Arrow* (publications) field, and all the office fields, and the ministry fields. I check every field and watch the Word of God grow and work and prosper and succeed in each of our endeavors.

You can be the same kind of farmer. The ministry happens to be my particular calling, but there is an arena and calling of life where you are. You have fields in which you are sowing seeds and you have things that you are watching grow. God wants your fields to be just as healthy and prosperous and flourishing and thriving as mine are, according to the Word.

> **Blessed shalt thou be in the city, and blessed shalt thou be in the field.**
> **Deuteronomy 28:3**

Marte and I have seen this thing work again and again and again. I told you it wasn't that big splash, but the constant drop of water on the rock that makes the difference. That continual day-in and day-out application of God's Word in your life will continually, daily, put you over. Success doesn't come from one day getting all hot and doing your best and the next day getting cold and not acting. Success comes from being single-minded, having singleness of purpose and being set on the Word of God. That is what attains the goal. Less, and you may fall short of the mark.

Your spirit man is like a great storehouse and a reservoir of the Spirit of God runs through you. If you decide to let God flow through you, creativity will begin flowing through you. You have that gift, but how often do you utilize it? Very seldom. But it's there all the time. It is the same in every aspect of the multi-faceted nature of God. It's there, but it is up to you and me to allow God's creativity to flow out.

God builds a strong desire in a particular area of your life. If you will begin to yield to that desire, that Godly desire, you will see that the Holy Spirit will begin to flow and you will become very strong and productive and a great blessing to the body of Christ in that area. That kind of person is a 100-fold productive Christian. That's not a one-fold, nor even a 30-fold. I believe God would be blessed with some 30-fold Christians and some 60-fold and really blessed with some 100-folds — those who are forgetting man's standards and looking at God's standards. I believe we are going to see some strong men and women in the last days. There haven't been many of them since the earth began. Really! There are going to be people who have gotten transfigured in the things of God.

> **Wherefore lay apart all filthiness and superfluity of naughtiness, and receive with meekness the engrafted word, which is able to save your souls.**
>
> **James 1:21**

The **engrafted word** sets you free. God's Word, understood, will free you from any restraint or restraining factors or situations. The Word will free you from any restraints.

> **But be ye doers of the word, and not hearers only, deceiving your own selves.**

For if any be a hearer of the word, and not a doer, he is like unto a man beholding his natural face in a glass:

For he beholdeth himself, and goeth his way, and straightway forgetteth what manner of man he was.
James 1:22-24

Here is a man who begins to look at himself and sees what kind of person he is. Then he goes away and forgets what kind of person he really is. And if your eye is evil, if you see only problems, that is all you will have. Your whole body will be full of darkness. Out of the abundance of the heart, the mouth will speak. So here is a man beholding himself. He is looking for the good, but he forgets, then goes his way, and he has deceived himself.

But out of the good treasures of the heart, a good man bringeth forth good things. The good man does this.

But whoso looketh into the perfect law of liberty, and continueth therein, he being not a forgetful hearer, but a doer of the work, this man shall be blessed in his deed.
James 1:25

This man is just like Jabez, who called on God, saying, **Oh that thou wouldst bless me in deed** (1 Chron. 4:10). And this man who looks through the perfect law of liberty is the man who will be blessed in his deed. We know in the Old Testament what Jabez did, but James writes under the New Testament and for the New Covenant time. He gives us an observation on how to be blessed in our deeds in the 20th century.

Perfect Law of Liberty

How are we blessed in our deeds today?

By looking through the perfect law of liberty. By seeing ourselves through the perfect law of liberty.

What is that perfect law of liberty?

First, it is Christ. Second, it is following the gospel. Third, it is the royal law of love. If you can't love your neighbor and your brothers and sisters whom you can see, how can you love God whom you cannot see?

We know that the key is looking or seeing through the law of liberty, being single-minded and single in purpose through the law of liberty. It is the Word, the promise of God, that is the foundation for expectations.

Let me define the word *law*. A law is a set of rules of conduct. Laws refer to statutes and ordinances and rules set down and enforced by a ruling authority. If we line up with rules and laws, they regulate our lives. A law regulates or rules. To *regulate* means "to make uniform or in harmony with standards." The perfect law of liberty is Christ and the gospel. The beatitudes, Jesus' Sermon on the Mount, is one way of looking at the perfect law of liberty. (Matt. 5:3-11.)

When we look through the perfect law of liberty, God's Law is regulating and ruling and guiding our lives for success, not failure. And if we continually behold and see through the perfect law of liberty, our entire lives and bodies will be full of light. Our lives will be ruled and regulated by God's Word, and we will always succeed, be happy, and have peace of mind.

God's Word contains the regulatory principles for success, happiness, and peace of mind. Anyone can try to attain them through his own works, but it is surely easier to do it through God's Word. It is simple through His Word. The perfect law of liberty is like a clock or watch. To adjust or regulate a clock, your standard is set for the speed of its turning. When our lives are in agreement and harmony with God, then our right standing with Him regulates the timepiece. We become on time and in agreement with God. And that regulatory law releases the life of God in our lives. When we are "on time," it releases the life of God to flow through us. And if we get out of love, the timepiece shuts down. It runs slow and gets all messed up.

Then there is that word *liberty* which means "to be free." God's rules and regulations free us from any restraints of lack or failure. Liberty means "to be free, to be released from slavery or enemy occupation, or any type of hindering stronghold." The perfect law of liberty releases the life of God out of our spirits. That is why it is extremely important to see and hear through the Word of God and to speak the Word of God. This must be our guideline and this is what will keep us on the road to success.

The word *look* also is in that verse — "that which sees or peers into." We want to see ourselves as God sees us. Then we will begin to act right. We don't want to be a person who beholds himself in a mirror and then goes away and forgets what kind of person he is.

Do you get a good picture from this of the kind of person you are? Then if you go out and begin to say things contrary to who you know you are, and say things under a facade of false humility, the Bible says that you deceive yourself and are double-minded. James says that a double-minded, or carnal-minded, person need not expect to receive anything from God.

That attitude just shuts down the flow from God. With God, you are delivered from failure, and your life becomes enjoyable. You can enjoy achievement and success. Without God, you just can't make it. With the flow from God, you can be an overcomer. You can see the difference in your own life. So choose life. Choose God!

2

ENERGIZING YOUR SPIRIT FOR CREATIVE RESULTS

Remember, the Kingdom of God **cometh not with observation,** but comes from looking at riches and success from God's point of view. It begins in the heart of man. **A good man out of the good treasure of his heart bringeth forth good things** (Matt. 12:35). The Kingdom of God is within you, and the Kingdom of God **cometh not with observation.** We are supposed to seek first the Kingdom of God and His righteousness. And *righteousness, peace, and joy* are found in the Holy Spirit.

We've learned that righteousness is being in right standing with God. Righteousness is being in harmony with the Creator of the universe. It's being an heir of God and a joint heir with Jesus. This righteousness causes us to enjoy the benefits which are prosperity and divine health and being delivered from a premature death.

God's laws or regulatory rules cause us to achieve our goals. *Righteousness* results in success and prosperity. *Peace* is having peace with God — peace in your heart and peace in your mind — and *joy* means happiness.

Now I want to share with you some information I've gleaned during the past several years. The Spirit of God has shown me these things. I believe, as E. W. Kenyon said, that success is here and readily available. And we are enjoying success at Word of Faith World Outreach Center. If you aren't a success, it's your fault, not God's. But I believe you are a success and that we are all growing.

The Word will work in anyone's life. The course of study in this book shows how to get hold of the Word. This course will help you eliminate frustrations, release more of Christ in your life, change your destiny, increase your creativity, help you deal wisely in all the affairs of life, and help you get things done. Would you like to see more things accomplished in your life? Are there things not done that you would like to see accomplished? This will help you learn how to get things done.

There is a key to getting things done: It's called *do it now*.

Procrastination Is the Thief of Time

Procrastination will steal time and prolong the job. I believe the teaching in this book will reinforce your desire or help you develop a strong enough desire and purpose to do the things you want to do.

Do you have strong desire and purpose in your life already for a particular attainment or some type of accomplishment? You may have a purpose that is scriptural and that you know God called you to do, but if your desire to fulfill that purpose is not strong enough, you won't persevere to the end and finish the course.

You are a God-kind of creature. You can accomplish things. You can enjoy accomplishment and fulfillment in your life. I believe this course will encourage you and inspire you to keep on and persevere in attaining the goal that you've set out to accomplish.

This course also will help you be more productive, enjoy more achievement and satisfaction, attain financial freedom, achieve personal success, and bring your life, ideas, feelings, and actions into harmony with God. It will help you change and be charged with the life of God. You will have more contentment and pleasure and enjoy divine health. You will inherit your inheritance and possess your possessions.

This is an informative introduction, designed to build a foundation so that you can take advantage of God's laws of success.

I counsel constantly with people who want to find out what we're doing in our ministry to cause the success we're having and how we receive all the things from God that we are receiving. Some write us, some call, and some come in person. Many of our visitors are ministers.

Our answer is simple. *We succeed because the Word is working in our lives.* We've gotten hold of the Word of God and are learning how to apply it in our lives. And we certainly have not cornered the market on it. God has shown us from His Word. We have worked the Word and the Word works! We enjoy the rewards of accomplishing things through God's Word. I believe that's scriptural and inspired of God. I don't believe our success is something that's man-made. I believe success is of God. In fact, God never made any failures. He wants everyone to be a success. Jesus came to deliver humanity from failure and bring us into success.

God has given us success, happiness, and peace of mind. We don't have to strive to attain them. We simply receive them by faith. There was a barrier separating God and man — the barrier of sin. But Jesus removed that barrier. He tore down the partition between God and man by satisfying the penalties of sin in His own body on the cross. If you have received Jesus' redemptive work at Calvary, there is no longer a barrier separating you from God. It has been removed. You have received the remitting of your sins and that removed the barrier between you and God the Father when you became born again in Christ.

Jesus is the Mediator — the Way, the Truth, and the Life. When you were born again, the Spirit of God came into your spirit and charged you with the life of God. Jesus delivered you from the condition of failure and brought you into a place of success. So understand and operate in and apply the principles of God's Word in your life. This will open up the rivers of life or the issues of life to flow from your spirit and cause everything you touch to live and to prosper. Everything we touch *shall* live and *shall* prosper with the Spirit of God and the nature of God flowing through us.

We Are New Creatures

You're a new creature, a God-kind of creature. **Old things are passed away; behold, all things are become new** (2 Cor. 5:17). As God's children, we are a new species on earth. We're like supermen. We are living in the Kingdom of God. Jesus Christ is living big in us, reigning and ruling in our lives. We have the Kingdom of God within us. Knowing this, how can there be any lack or shortage in our lives? How can there be any sickness or any type of lack of vitality in us?

Jesus delivered you from a condition of failure and brought you into a place of success! Understanding and applying God's principles will open the rivers of life to you and cause that life to flow from your spirit. Everything you touch should prosper.

You should be walking with God every minute of every day, allowing His Spirit to energize your thoughts and actions. The key to enjoying a 100 percent walk with God is allowing His Word to operate in you so that you can come into harmony with Him.

> **But whoso looketh into the perfect law of liberty, and continueth therein, he being not a forgetful hearer, but a doer of the work, this man shall be blessed in his deed.**
>
> **James 1:25**

Just as Moses lifted up the brazen serpent upon the pole, Jesus was lifted up. Jesus said, **And I, if I be lifted up from the earth, will draw all men unto me** (John 12:32). The way Jesus was lifted up is the same way that we look upon Him through the gospel. **Whoso looketh into the perfect law of liberty** — the law of liberty was Jesus' perfect redemptive work at Calvary and in His resurrection.

The gospel is that perfect law of liberty. Jesus preached the gospel, the good news of setting humanity free. He liberated us. He preached the acceptable year of the Lord. (Luke 4:19.) The perfect law of liberty is the Word of God. Look unto Jesus, the author and the finisher of our faith. (Heb. 12:2.) Look unto Jesus and what He did for us and through us, and what He is doing inside of us today. He brings a release and freedom in our lives unparalleled by anything except what we receive through the presence of God.

This perfect law of liberty is the gospel of Jesus Christ. Jesus preached the good news to set the captives free. He preached liberty. Jesus said in John 8:31,32, **If ye continue in my word, then are ye my disciples indeed; And ye shall know the truth, and the truth shall make you free.**

I believe, according to the Word, we are the disciples of Christ. We are continuing in the Word of God. Because of that, a special blessing is on our lives. God shows us special partiality. God affords us special privileges as long as we continue in His Word.

But whoso looketh into the perfect law of liberty . . . shall be blessed in his deed. The law is like a rule or a regulation. The Word of God regulates and rules us and brings us into success. The Word of God regulates and guides our lives for success. It causes divine care, favor, and friendly partiality to be invoked upon us. It brings a manifestation of God's blessings upon us. Spending time in God's Word is spending time with Him. Allowing Jesus to be Lord in our lives is allowing the Word to be Lord.

God wants His people to know success. I cannot stress this fact enough. He has a special formula or principle for energizing your spirit so that you can experience the success that already belongs to you through the New Covenant. God has a secret formula for seeding your spirit, for feeding and energizing your spirit man. This is found in Joshua.

> **This book of the law shall not depart out of thy mouth; but thou shalt meditate therein day and night, that thou mayest observe to do according to all that is written therein: for then thou shalt make thy way prosperous, and then thou shalt have good success.**
> **Joshua 1:8**

God is speaking here to Joshua, the man God had appointed to continue Moses' ministry. God raised up Joshua to bring the children of Israel into the Promised Land — the inheritance promised them through father Abraham. Joshua 1:8 contains instructions that God Himself was giving to His servant Joshua. These instructions were the source of his strength and courage in bringing the children of Israel into the Promised Land. It takes the power and the strength of God to lead His people!

God said, . . . **but thou shalt meditate therein day and night, that thou mayest observe to do according to all that is written therein: for** *then* **thou shalt make thy way prosperous, and** *then* **thou shalt have good success.** These instructions are very simple and precise. *If* you follow through with them, *then* your re-created spirit will be energized to operate as God intends.

What you want to see reproduced in your life must be first planted in your spirit. Only when you sow the proper seeds can there be any reproduction or bringing forth. Implant the incorruptible seed of God's Word in your spirit. When you do, it will start working in your life. You will become so fired up that all you'll have to do is keep it watered. It will work for you night and day. **This book of the law** (God's regulations for success) **shall not depart out of thy mouth.**

In other words, *whatever you do, allow only God's words to come forth from your mouth.* Don't allow any type of corrupt communication to come out of your mouth. Only speak God's words. Don't let other words get in your mouth. Just speak God's Word.

There are three elements involved in God's formula for success. They are *information, meditation, and application.* Before we have finished this lesson, I'll tell you how to write down the things you've been believing for from God. A petition is something written down to present to an authority. And you will need to write down some of your petitions. If you haven't seen the fulfillment of some of the things you've been believing God for, you'll need to double up on energizing your spirit with the substance of those things hoped for. I will show you how to do that. I will show you how to plant in your spirit what you want to see reproduced. If there is no sowing, there can't be any reproducing or bringing forth.

You are a free moral agent with the power of choice over what goes into your spirit. You must choose and you must decide. *You must decide what you want or you will have to settle for whatever you get!*

Information Is Knowledge Received

Information is knowledge received concerning a particular fact or circumstance. The word *information* comes from the word *inform*. This book will inform you about what you can receive from God. Information comes as knowledge acquired by reading, observation, and studying. There is nothing wrong with watching someone else. A wise man associates with other wise men and becomes wiser himself. This is why I travel. From time to time, I spend several hours with someone I consider to be wise for I enjoy being with other successful people. In fact, I'll help someone become a success who has been a failure, but I don't associate with failures who are content to remain failures. I try to associate with successful people in the ministry and successful businessmen and women.

The book of the Law is the information. The Bible is the book of success. It's your information source. If you're having problems in some area, if you're not seeing what you desire come to pass, get the Bible and a concordance. Find in God's book what you need to receive. That's your book of information. You must get information.

Success involves attaining a particular goal or accomplishment. You could say it means inheriting the promises of God's Word and receiving the results hoped for. A success turns out as planned. It has a favorable outcome. Failure is falling short of the mark.

Of course, we all **press toward the mark for the prize of the high calling of God in Christ Jesus** (Phil. 3:14) — which is to be like Jesus Christ. That is the ultimate. I believe we're all ripening like fruit on a tree. The Lord showed me in my spirit that we're getting sweeter every day. We are just getting sweeter every day. I believe I'm getting sweeter every day. Aren't you glad we're becoming more like Him every day?

Information is the first element involved in God's formula for success. This comes from the word *inform*. Let's talk for a moment about being informed. Information coming to you can cause you to be inspired in that particular area. For example, as you read scriptures on the subject of healing, you're planting those scriptures into your spirit. When you acquire that information or knowledge, you become informed; then you become inspired in that particular area.

A woman from Ohio who had an open tumor on her breast is a good example of the inspiration of information. She'd been sent home by doctors to die and heard me through our radio broadcast in her area. She ordered some of our "faith-food" tapes. Then she called me and said, "They don't work!" But I told her not to ever again call me and talk like that because she was being disrespectful — not to me, but to God. "The Word of God does work," I told her, "and don't you ever say that again!"

I told her to play those tapes again and again and to listen and meditate on the scriptures until she got healed. If she wore out the tapes, I told her we'd send her some more. A few weeks later, she called back shouting the praises of God. She had done exactly as I told her and was healed. I had straightened out her thinking. She was used to telling everyone else what to do, but I told her what she needed to do. Some folks are too hard-headed to listen to anyone else. They want the answer but won't listen to anyone who tries to give it to them. I was nice to her, but I told her the truth and she received it! She was totally delivered of that tumor because **faith cometh by hearing, and hearing by the word of God** (Rom. 10:17).

Several people have been healed of hypoglycemia at Word of Faith. Not many people get healed of hypoglycemia, but God set them free because His Word is alive. Hebrews 4:12 says, **The word of God is quick, and powerful, and sharper than any two-edged sword.** The word *quick* means alive. That means it's charged with life. Not just everyday life, it's charged with the life of God. In the original Greek translation, *zoe* is the word used. God's Word is alive with *zoe* — the very life and nature of God. It is quick (alive). The Word of God is powerful. That is the Greek word *dunamis*, like dynamite.

This book of the law shall not depart out of thy mouth. In other words, keep the Word of God in your mouth. This isn't some science of mind or religious science doctrine. This is Christian sense. This is the Word of God. You'll catch flack from people for talking God's talk. And here's why: So few people are talking God's talk that they think something is wrong with you when you do. But this concept is just exploding. People all over the world are now preaching the Word of God and the word of faith.

> **But what saith it? The word is nigh thee, even in thy mouth, and in thy heart: that is, the word of faith, which we preach.**
>
> **Romans 10:8**

If you're preaching the Bible, you're preaching faith and it will produce results. *Faith produces results.*

You know, if there's a congregation or a family that's not having any results in the Christian life, something is wrong. For the Word, when continually fed upon, will bring results in your life — in your business, in your ministry, in any facet of your life. God created everything to produce after its own kind. And the Word will produce in your life, if you will take the time to plant it and water it. The Word will produce in your life.

Some people are good farmers because they take the time to be. My granddad was a good farmer. He sowed and he took good care of his crops, doing what he was supposed to do. As good Christians, we should take heed to the way good farmers take care of their crops. As believers, we should take care how we feed ourselves the Word of God. We need it every day. We must read it and study it every day.

I like what Smith Wigglesworth said, "Most Christians feed their bodies three hot meals a day and feed their spirits one cold snack a week. Then they wonder why they don't get anything from God." We aren't that way, are we? And we get some criticism for not being like that! That is because we are salty. If you're not salty, you're good for nothing, spiritually. But you *are* good for something, aren't you? You are the light of the world, a candle set on a hill.

You are a lighthouse, and those groping in darkness will see that light coming out of you. Those looking for the light shall be drawn to you. Many people are hungry for righteousness. That simply means they are hungry to be in right standing with God. They don't want to be foreigners, alienated from their Creator. People are hungry. And you have the light of all lights, and you have the influence of God beaming from your life.

Desire without knowledge is not good. On our road of success, Marte and I have encountered people who failed to achieve the things they were believing God for. We've seen people who wanted to go into the ministry. They wanted to do things for God. And we've seen some of them attempt to do those things. But because they lacked knowledge and understanding to accompany their desire, they failed. Some of them now have shipwrecked faith. You must have more than just the desire to accomplish a certain thing. The Bible advises this:

> **Study to shew thyself approved unto God, a workman that needeth not to be ashamed, rightly dividing the word of truth.**
>
> **2 Timothy 2:15**

There's a prudence in preparing yourself for the things you desire to do and receive. There is a preparation period. Training is involved. You don't just jump into the cockpit of an airplane and take off. First, you receive some training. The same principle applies to developing your spirit in the things you're believing God for. A prize fighter trains and develops his muscles. He builds himself by feeding on the right foods.

Should we as believers do any less spiritually? No! We are in training. We need to work out with the Word of God. We should get up in the morning, open our Bibles to the promises we are believing God for, and begin to speak the Word of God against those mountains of problems. We need to speak God's Word against the giants in our lives. We need to work out really good every morning.

If it just takes doing that, do it. If you need healing say, *"Devil, by the stripes of Jesus, I am healed!"* If you need finances, say this:

> *I have plenty of money in the bank for God is not holding it back. There is no poverty in heaven. I have prayed that God's will be done on earth as it is in heaven, and it's not God holding it back. I receive my finances because I bind the devil and loose the angels to bring it in. I thank You, Father God, that I have more than enough to support any ministry that is preaching the gospel and setting the captives free, with enough left over to pay all my bills at the end of the month. I have enough to bless my family because I seek first the Kingdom of God. I am prospering. Praise Your name!*
>
> *I thank You, God, that I'm not down in the dumps. I'm not crawling like a worm on the floor. I thank You that I've been delivered, oh, God, from sorrow and grief and depression. I've been elevated and raised up with Jesus. I have a sound mind. I don't have a spirit of fear. Hallelujah! I'm the righteousness of God. I am bold as a lion. Hallelujah!*

Did you know that you forget perhaps 25 percent of the information that you hear or read within about 24 hours? By reviewing that information, you can greatly improve this rate. Reviewing, re-reading notes taken at a meeting, and meditating on the material greatly improves memory. I know the Holy Spirit can cause things to be remembered, but I believe we must also do what we know to do. Reviewing is the most valuable, and perhaps the most neglected, learning skill.

At times I listen to a good tape 10 to 20 times until it gets down into my spirit. Material to be learned usually must be reviewed several times before it really becomes part of your spirit.

Meditate for Understanding

Let's now look at meditation. Joshua 1:8 is also a good scripture on meditation. It's perhaps the foundational scripture on meditation in the Word.

> **This book of the law shall not depart out of thy mouth; but thou shalt meditate therein day and night, that thou mayest observe to do according to all that is written therein: for then thou shalt make thy way prosperous, and then thou shalt have good success** (deal wisely).

This scripture says, **Meditate. . .that thou mayest observe to do.** In other words, meditating gives you understanding of how to apply God's Word in your life. You can memorize scriptures, but that's not enough. You have to know how to apply them in your life — how to act on them and speak them. You must believe that God's Word will do for you what He said it will do.

Someone I know had a lot of scriptures memorized, but didn't know how to apply them in life or how to speak in faith. But when this person started attending Word of Faith, he asked a lot of questions.

Once in awhile, he would skin his knees, spiritually speaking. But he got back up again and kept going. He knew it was the truth, and he wasn't going to depart from it. He may have had a few pains and sores, but God healed them every time. He started growing. He didn't stop. He believed that God's Word would do what God said it would, and he learned how to apply the scriptures that he knew.

I am that way. I have had opportunities to give up and be a failure. There have been more opportunities to miss God and fail than you could imagine. But I kept seeing myself the way God sees me. I wouldn't let God's Word depart from my mouth. I kept speaking God's Word instead of speaking failure, lack, and poverty. I kept saying it as God said to say it.

People have said of me, "Oh, he's just one of those faith guys. He thinks he can have what he says." That's right. I sure do! And I don't mind telling you so. People also have said, "Oh, it's just a fad. It's just a passing fancy." No. It's truth, and it's taking over the whole world. God is raising up a new breed. God is raising up a strong people in these last days, strong faith men and women turned on to the promises of God's Word. A people who are not taking any flack from the devil.

Some people say, "Well, we have to have a balance." The balance they talk about has them taking flack from the devil. I'm not taking anything from the devil! And I'm not giving up anything to him, either.

Even if I find myself preaching the Word to only one person, I won't change what I'm preaching. I don't preach this just because it's popular, either. I preached it when nobody came. I preached it when I had more money at the start of meetings than I did when I left the meetings. But I kept preaching it because I wasn't going to compromise, and I wasn't going to change what God had showed me in His Word.

I started catching hold. The Word worked. You know, I could be a success anywhere I am with God's Word in my spirit. I don't have to just be at a church to achieve success. God's Word will work for you and me anywhere. When you get success principles into your spirit, it doesn't make a whole lot of difference what you're doing. You will know how to do it. So you might as well decide on something you enjoy and like, right? I refuse to compromise or change what God showed me in His Word.

Success is inevitable, once you get the principles of God's Word into your spirit. The Word will work for you anywhere at any time. If you don't enjoy your job, you ought to say, "Father, I make a petition that You will give me work where I can utilize the talents that You designed me for." Start confessing it and believing it. Just watch. God will open doors for you, and you'll go through those doors.

I don't know why some people live their whole lives doing things they don't like to do. That is a waste of your life. If I stepped on your toes, I'm sorry. But I want you to grow even more, and I want you to enjoy what Jesus died to give you.

I used to be a draftsman and there's nothing wrong with being a draftsman, but I wanted to build houses. And I just believed myself into a good job. They made me a deal I couldn't refuse. But I wanted to build houses, and I just believed myself into it. I just said, "God, I thank You that You give me the desires of my heart." (Ps. 37.)

Perhaps you are being ministered to specifically with this word. You have really been discouraged in a particular area of life. Accept this word. Claim it for yourself. But don't go out and quit your present job tomorrow. Use prudence. Good wisdom is to believe God for a better job to come in and then quit your present job.

Application of the Word of God

Our three points are *information, meditation, and application.* Joshua 1:8 is the text for this third point as well. First, you take God's Book of the Law, His Information and Promises for Success. Secondly, you become informed. Do not let God's Word depart out of your mouth. Keep it in your mouth, your speech. Then you **meditate therein day and night.**

Last of all comes application. **That thou mayest *observe to do* according to all that is written therein: for then thou shalt make thy way prosperous, and then thou shalt have good success.** In modern English, you will make your way prosperous through the Word of God (or, rather, the Word will do it through you), if you will apply the Word. You have a part to play. After you get the information into your spirit by meditation, then you have to put it to work in your life. *You have to do the work.*

In South Africa, the larger industries want Christians to work for them. Christians there don't steal. They come to work every day and they are loyal, trustworthy employees who work hard. I believe it is going to be this way in the United States in these last days. I believe you are worthy of a good salary, because you don't waste your time, you aren't off on sick leave, and you don't gossip and breed strife at work. I believe employers will see that you do your job and control your tongue, and they'll reward you for it.

Once the Word of God is operative in your life, then you'll be successful, then you'll make your way prosperous. The Word will work through you and bring prosperity and success. I don't know about you, but I like my way being prosperous. When I get up every morning, I say something like this:

> *Lord, I thank You that the Word is working mightily inside me. I thank You that everything we do and everything we put our hands to is prospering. I thank You, Father God, that our call is to the Church, to minister to Your people. I thank You, Father God, for an overwhelming anointing this morning; for the largest attendance yet at our church; for all our bills to be met, with money left over.*

It seems every week our attendance grows larger, and every week God brings forth new revelation knowledge and nuggets of truth to feed His people. Every week the income of the church is growing larger than ever.

I have prophesied from the pulpit, and continue to prophesy that we're going to be pulling in so many fish in these last days that our nets will begin to break. We will have to cry out to other boats — other churches will have to come and help us bring in the fish! *We'll have to start sending people over to other churches that are preaching the Word.*

You may say, "I never heard of anything like that."

You haven't been living in the last of the last days before. That is what will happen in the days to come. People will be coming to us from all over the world and going out from us to all the world, prophesying and speaking God's Word, preaching God's Word, and speaking the Word of faith.

That is exciting to anticipate. I look forward to it. I enjoy things like that.

> **Hear, ye children, the instruction of a father, and attend to know understanding.**
>
> **For I give you good doctrine, forsake ye not my law.**
>
> **For I was my father's son, tender and only beloved in the sight of my mother.**
>
> **He taught me also, and said unto me, Let thine heart retain my words: keep my commandments, and live.**
>
> **Get wisdom, get understanding: forget it not; neither decline from the words of my mouth.**
>
> **Forsake her not, and she shall preserve thee: love her, and she shall keep thee.**
>
> **Wisdom is the principal thing; therefore get wisdom: and with all thy getting get understanding.**
>
> **Exalt her, and she shall promote thee: she shall bring thee to honour, when thou dost embrace her.**
>
> **She shall give to thine head an ornament of grace: a crown of glory shall she deliver to thee.**
>
> **Hear, O my son, and receive my sayings; and the years of thy life shall be many.**
>
> **Proverbs 4:1-10**

Your heart receives the implanted Word of God, and your heart is your spirit. This scripture says to get wisdom and get understanding. Knowledge is good, but get understanding with it. Understand what you're getting. It's better to get a little bit and understand it than to get a whole lot and not understand any of it.

Keep my commandments, and live (v. 4). To keep them is to act on them, to do them, and to honor them. **Forsake her not, and she shall preserve thee: love her, and she shall keep thee** (v. 7). The Word with understanding will keep you. It will keep your life from the corruption of this world.

Wisdom (the Word) **shall bring thee to honour, when thou dost embrace her** (v. 8). How close to a person are you when you embrace? That is how close you must be to the Word to embrace it. Then **she shall give to thine head an ornament of grace:** (or favor) (and) **a crown of glory** (high rank and honor) **shall she deliver to thee** (v. 9).

Receive my sayings; and the years of thy life shall be many (v. 10). That is divine health. Lives are being prolonged today because people are receiving the instructions of God's Word. You might as well receive that promise. Then your years shall be many.

Here is a confession for you to say aloud so you will hear these words in your own voice:

> *I receive instruction from God's Word. Therefore, my years shall be many — productive and flourishing years, rewarding years, fulfilling years, enjoyable years upon this earth. I receive enjoyment and pleasure in doing the Word of God. I have a purpose. I am single-minded, not double-minded. I speak only God's Word, and I think only upon God's thoughts. Therefore my way is prosperous. My way is succeeding, thriving, and growing vigorously. I am growing vigorously. I am filled with life. When a trial comes against my faith, I always have the strength to resist it. Praise God!*

Vigorous means "full of vitality and life." That is why you can say, "I am filled with life."

> **I have taught thee in the way of wisdom; I have led thee in right paths.**
>
> **When thou goest, thy steps shall not be straitened; and when thou runnest, thou shalt not stumble.**
> **Proverbs 4:11,12**

Oh, I like that. Those verses say that you don't fall along the way and have to get up and dust yourself off. By receiving the instruction and wisdom and good understanding from God's Word, the path will be straight when you walk. And you will not stumble when you run. Does that minister life to you? It does to me. *To straiten* means "to make narrow." It refers to difficulties in your path. First we receive God's instruction, and then we allow Him to lead us in right paths. That means we act, doesn't it? That means we walk the right walk and will not fall along the way or stumble down a narrow, difficult path.

Stating this principle in the positive, Soloman says in verse 12: **when thou runnest . . . .** How do we travel? What are the **right paths** like? They aren't narrow and restricted by obstacles. And we don't stumble for there is nothing to stumble over — except perhaps our own sometimes stubborn feet.

> **Take fast hold of instruction; let her not go: keep her; for she is thy life.**
>
> **Proverbs 4:13**

What is **thy life?** Instructions. **Thy life** is dependent upon instruction. Don't let the devil talk you out of going to church services. Don't miss out. Don't let even other good activities keep you away. This doesn't mean just your physical presence at church. Come to receive instructions. Get under the ministry of the Word of God. Stay under it. You need to receive instruction. Get under the ministry of the anointed Word and stay under it. The pastor's job is to put the Word into you, not to exalt himself, philosophies, or denominations. Get the Word of God. You need it. It is your life.

Sometimes people say, "You bet your life!" It is your life at stake. Receive instruction from the Word of God. He is doing a quick work today. This is a new day. He is doing a new thing. The whole body is being trained by God's fullness of teaching: apostles, prophets, evangelists, pastors, and teachers. (Eph. 4:11.) They are ministering to God's people. God is using them to do a quick work. Whatever your pastor doesn't know, God sends someone else in who does know. So you can get God's revelation knowledge and feed on it and get it working down in your spirit.

The Word of God is literally pulling up, by the roots, some strongholds that have been in cities and nations for years. The Word of God is burning out all the junk and is setting the believers and the captives free. It is enlightening and strengthening believers all across the world. **Exalt her, and she shall promote thee** (v. 8).

I just want you turned on to the Word. I don't care how you get there. Just get there. Get turned on to the Word of God. When you're full of the Word, you will affect the people around you. You will win souls for the Lord. When you're filled with the Holy Spirit, you cannot shut your mouth, **for out of the abundance of the heart the mouth speaketh** (Matt. 12:34). You have to tell how God and His Word are working in your life. You get to be a fanatic around everyone you meet. You're compelled to tell them about the Word working in your life.

There is something different about turned-on believers. They just stand out. The life of God shines through their spirits. God's glory shines. Believers shine with His glory. Make this confession aloud: "I am shining with His glory! I'm shining with the glory of the Lord."

Enter not into the path of the wicked, and go not in the way of evil men.

Avoid it, pass not by it, turn from it, and pass by.

Proverbs 4:14,15

Who wants to go in the way of evil men? They don't know what they're doing. They are walking in darkness. The Bible says, **If the blind lead the blind, both shall fall into the ditch** (Matt. 15:14). God doesn't want His people following blind leaders. What would happen? They both fall in the ditch.

> **For they sleep not, except they have done mischief; and their sleep is taken away, unless they cause some to fall.**
>
> **For they eat the bread of wickedness, and drink the wine of violence.**
>
> **But the path of the just is as the shining light, that shineth more and more unto the perfect day.**
>
> **The way of the wicked is as darkness: they know not at what they stumble.**
>
> **Proverbs 4:16-19**

Notice the contrast between the path (the directions) of the just and the way of the wicked. We can say this confession:

> *I am shining more and more and more every day unto the perfect day. The glory of the Lord, shining from within me, is getting brighter every day. I am getting brighter every day. It may be getting darker in the outside world, but I am getting brighter on the inside. My path is in the shining light. I run fast and never stumble.*
>
> *For those in the world, it's getting darker. The world is approaching total darkness, and worldly people stumble and they know not at what they stumble.*

Now we come to a passage that is among the most famous in the Bible: **My son, attend to my words; incline thine ear unto my sayings** (v. 20). Only your true father can call you, **My son.** *To attend* is "to pay attention, to heed," or "to have your full awareness focused upon something." You could say *to attend* means "to study."

Next He says **incline thine ear unto my sayings.** That obviously means to listen to what God has to say. In order to listen to His sayings, your own voice should be speaking God's sayings. There's nothing wrong with people telling you something, as long as you know that it's scriptural. If it's not, don't listen to them. Don't "attend to their words." You can love them. You don't have "to clobber" them with your spiritual insight. But don't receive what they're saying if it's not from God.

Keep looking at the Word (the sayings): **Let them not depart from thine eyes; keep them in the midst of thine heart** (v. 21). Keep looking into the perfect law of liberty. Keep seeing yourself the way God sees you. See yourself identified with Jesus in His death, burial, and resurrection. See yourself seated with Christ in a position of power and authority. See yourself seated in a heavenly position with Christ. That changes everything.

As long as the devil has you crawling around like a worm in a pile of dust, you won't get anything from God. Start seeing what God has given you through Jesus. It will change everything you do. It will change your life. You can't help being successful, if you will do these basic things.

Verse 21 concludes: **Keep them** (God's sayings) **in the midst of thine heart.** Your heart, your spirit, is where you deposit the sayings of God. Your heart is designed to reproduce exactly what is sown in it. If you've been putting trash there, that's what you have been reproducing. If you desire more good to come out of your heart, then you must sow more of God's thoughts and words into your heart. To see more success, put more and more of the Word within you. The Word brings success.

> **For they are life unto those that find them, and health to all their flesh.**
>
> **Keep thy heart with all diligence; for out of it are the issues of life.**
>
> **Proverbs 4:22,23**

The root of the word *meditate* is the same as the root of the words *medical* and *medicine*. It means "to measure" or "to consider." And on the medical side of the word, doctors "considered" working on the physical persons. *Meditate* also means "to ponder or think upon, to consider, plan or think." And we want to ponder, think upon, and consider God's ways and His words. *Meditate* can mean "to mutter, to speak under one's breath, or to talk." Why ought we to speak God's Word? Because faith — a spiritual substance — faith as a seed is sown in your heart. And when you hear God's Word, it gets sown down in your spirit.

Faith is sown as a seed in your heart when you hear the Word of God. You feed your spirit by hearing God's Word. God gave you ears not only to communicate with other people, but also for the feeding of your own spirit — to hear God's Word.

I like what Charles Capps said. He says you have an inner ear and an outer ear. Whether or not you realize it, you hear your own voice through the inner ear. You do not hear what you sound like to the outer ear. Charles Capps believes — and it make sense — that the inner ear is for speaking God's Word and feeding your spirit. The Bible is clear — you feed your spirit by hearing God's Word. God gave you ears to communicate with other people but also for the feeding of your spirit through hearing His Word.

Blessed is the man that walketh not in the counsel of the ungodly, nor standeth in the way of sinners, nor sitteth in the seat of the scornful.

But his delight is in the law of the Lord; and in his law doth he meditate day and night.

And he shall be like a tree planted by the rivers of water, that bringeth forth his fruit in his season; his leaf also shall not wither; and whatsoever he doeth shall prosper.

Psalm 1:1-3

Blessed or highly favored is the man whose delight is in God's Law (regulations for success). He meditates day and night in God's Law. When you meditate and ponder upon God's Word, you are **like a tree planted by the rivers of water** (v. 3). In Hebrew, that means the delta land where many rivers come together. They deposit sediment that is highly fertile soil. You are like a tree planted in that highly concentrated fertile soil.

And you will spring up and bring forth fruit in your season. You will prosper, thrive, and grow vigorously. Meditating in the Word will bring forth the fruit of God's Word. Meditating in God's Word will release the substance of things hoped for and cause them to become a reality in your life. Then whatever you do will prosper because you have the guideline or regulation or programming for success. If you're regulated and programmed for success through God's Word, how can you steer off the path? You will run and not stumble. For the path is brightly lighted by the Light of life, God's Word. The Holy Spirit is your guide. You will succeed and not fail. You will thrive and flourish.

Your leaf will not wither. Whatever you do will prosper. Why? Because you are programmed to succeed.

God's Word is designed to work and to accomplish what it was sent forth to accomplish. It will never return to Him void. It will always prosper. It will always thrive. It will always do what God desired it to do. Think about it. Put it down into your spirit. And then the fruit of your mouth — your speech — releases it here in the earth.

We have just begun to operate by the guidelines of faith. We have just begun to see what God will do through us by His Word. And I am enjoying every minute of it. Aren't you? I like it.

How to Feed and Energize Your Spirit

1. *Decide what you want to plant in your spirit.* You have the power of choice to decide what you're going to feed upon. Whatever you plant and water will come up. It will produce. Do you know of some things you wish to see come to pass in your life?

This is a way to really strengthen and reinforce what you've been believing God for. Right away, get a small notebook or some 3-by-5 cards. I have a notebook in which I have written down the things for which I am believing God. And I write down the people I have to see, the ideas, and the different departments that we are working on, as well.

2. *Write as briefly as possible one thing you're believing God for. That's called a petition. Write each petition on a separate card.* Seeing what you have written helps to reinforce your petition. Cards have one advantage over

note books. You can easily carry them with you throughout the day as a reminder.

3. *Beneath your petition, write out the scripture or scriptures which substantiate why you can believe you are going to receive that particular thing from God.* Underline it in red for further emphasis. You may say, "Bob, this is simple." Yes it is. But how many people are missing it and not receiving most of the time?

Now that you have backed up your petition with a scripture, this petition becomes believable. If it's not backed up by scripture, then it's not believable. Unless it is believable, you won't have the strength to believe that you have received it. Only when it becomes believable to you will you possess the spiritual strength to endure storms and attacks from Satan, who tries to keep you from receiving it.

If the world is smart and accomplishes things, how much more should Christians accomplish things? But many Christians are just big old babies. Really! And they look for a sign and put out a fleece — and get fleeced. Often they give up before the race is even started. It's true! I've seen devils with more intestinal fortitude than a lot of Christians. And we've already read the Book of Revelation and know that we have won!

Some say, "Well, this won't work. It's just too hard." Who said that? Who said it won't work? Who said it was too hard? It's not too hard, and it does work. That's why I'm taking the time to make it clear for you.

And this is the confidence that we have in him, that, if we ask any thing according to his will, he heareth us:

And if we know that he hear us, whatsoever we ask, we know that we have the petitions that we desired of him.

1 John 5:14,15

4. *Now take the card and look at it. Read it aloud. Every morning when you get up, take the card and read it aloud. Say, "Father, I thank You that I receive* (insert whatever you're believing for), *according to Your Word." Then shut your eyes and see yourself with the answer, through the eye of faith.*

God told Joshua how to be strong, then He turned him loose. But, first, He turned Joshua's face toward Jericho and said, **See, I have given into thine hand Jericho, and the king thereof, and the mighty men of valour** (Josh. 6:2). If Joshua had gone by natural eyes, he would have seen those big thick walls and those men with swords and armament. It would've looked like he couldn't receive that city. But because he was built up in his spirit, this promise was believable to Joshua. He believed that he could receive the city of Jericho — so he did.

Take what you believe you received, and the scripture. By saying it out loud and meditating upon it — muttering it, seeing yourself receiving that promise — you are feeding it into your spirit, and you are storing it up in your treasure chest. Once that implanted Word is placed inside. You can know you have received. The Bible says that God *has given* us these exceedingly great and precious promises:

According as his divine power hath given unto us all things that pertain unto life and godliness, through the knowledge of him that hath called us to glory and virtue:

> **Whereby are given unto us exceeding great and precious promises: that by these ye might be partakers of the divine nature, having escaped the corruption that is in the world through lust.**
>
> **2 Peter 1:3,4**

To partake also means "to take portions of something." By feeding on the Word of God (depositing the Word into our spirits), we take portions of the nature and the Spirit of God and deposit them down into the good soil of our heart. We contain portions of the nature of God on the inside of us! It's alive, it's powerful, and it's sharper than any two-edged sword. (Heb. 4:12.) It will put you over and bring you into success every time.

By seeing and reading your card several times daily, you are feeding that information into your spirit and storing it up.

5. *Now memorize the scripture and say it to yourself.* Hear yourself say it. Speak it aloud until it gets down into your spirit. Once it is sown, it's just a matter of saying, *"Father, I thank You that I believe I have received* _____." Then corresponding actions of inspired thoughts will cause the words to become a reality.

Now you have information and meditation. Next, you need the application. Take the first step toward believing you received whatever you're believing God for. Many times, all you can see is the next step. If you see only one single step of faith to take, then take that single step and then believe for the following step.

If God had told me in the beginning of my ministry to come to the location where we are now and said, "There you are going to have 40,000 people going to church and you are going to have much of the acreage and property in that area and have buildings all over the place," I would probably have passed out. But I saw all I could see at the time. God told Abraham, **For all the land which thou seest, to thee will I give it** (Gen. 13:15). At the time we moved to the site where Word of Faith is now, my faith was just developed to the point of getting here. It took all the faith we had just to get here and get a place to meet. But we went that far.

So do whatever you can do. Take whatever step you can toward what you believe you have received. The first step most of us need to take is to get as much information and understanding as possible concerning what we're believing God for. **With all thy getting get understanding** (Prov. 4:7). I'm not saying to throw away your glasses or flush your medicine away. I'm saying, take whatever first step of faith you can take. And one early step of faith that we can take is to begin confessing God's Word. If you need new tires on your car, say something like this:

> *Father, I thank You for the new tires on my car, because You said that You wanted me to prosper. And You said in Philippians that You supply all of my need. And Father, that car needs some tires. Father, I thank You that those tires are supplied upon my car.*

Then you have to figure out what kind of tires your car takes. That's the next step of faith — what size tires do you have to have? What kind do you need? Radials? Nylon? Next, you say, "I thank You, Father, that I received them." The succeeding step of faith may be to price a few tires and write the basic cost on your card. Then say, "Father, I thank You that I believe I receive these tires or the finances to purchase these tires."

If that is as far as you can go, just keep watering that seed. I want you to know that everything produces after its own kind. And somewhere within the next few days or several weeks or whenever, somehow those tires will be reproduced and manifested for you. You say, "Bob, are they going to fall down from heaven?" No! In some way or another, you're going to get some tires. You may have to pay for them, but you'll have the money. This process looses it. Acting on the Word of God begins to loose the answer to prayer for you.

After information, meditation, and application, then just thank God for giving you whatever it is you need. Then all you can do is keep watering that seed. I want you to remember that everything reproduces after its own kind, and somewhere within the next few days or weeks (in God's perfect timing), you will receive.

When you begin to act on the Word of God, your action looses whatever it is you need. I don't want you to think of your past failures. I want you to forget all the times you've missed it and all the times you didn't receive. Forget them. Discard them. Start fresh right now, like you'd never started before. I want you to forget any negative thoughts of not having it or not being able to make it. You can make it. In fact, the Word of God will make you make it. Just feed your spirit the Word. Water it — think upon it. Say it. Take what steps you can.

If you don't have another step to take and you've done all, then just stand. (Eph. 6:13.) Keep the seed of the Word watered. Keep saying it. And that Word will keep growing. It might be five years. So what? It still works.

> **But let patience have her perfect work, that ye may be perfect and entire** (or complete), **wanting nothing.**
> **James 1:4**

Cast not away therefore your confidence, which hath great recompence of reward.

Hebrews 10:35

Let us hold fast the profession of our faith without wavering; (for he is faithful that promised.)

Hebrews 10:23

There is a story about Conrad Hilton who became one of the wealthiest people in the world. He failed and went bankrupt several times. He borrowed money to barely make it. But he didn't give up because he knew his idea was right. He wouldn't give up, and he became wealthy.

Walt Disney was broke several times and owed money all over the place. But he knew he had a good idea, and he didn't let lack of money stop him. He kept going forward when everything looked as if he couldn't make it. And eventually he succeeded, because faith is like a seed. It will grow if you continue to act upon it.

Shoot for the stars and watch God bring things to pass in your life that you never thought possible. They are possible in these last days. *All* things are possible with God!

3

OBTAINING THE UNOBTAINABLE

Heavenly Father, I thank You for the anointing that abides within my spirit man — a very special anointing that You placed within my heart when I yielded to the call You put upon my life to minister the gospel of the Lord Jesus Christ. Father, I expect that anointing to do supernatural things. I expect Your Word to come out of me and be anointed. I expect the reader to be able to understand. By faith, I receive everything You have for me and for the reader. God, teach us how to be successful in life. As we hear Your Word, we will take portions of Your Spirit and deposit them into our hearts. And they will reproduce themselves here in this earth. I thank You, Father, for that and declare it done through the Name of Jesus. Amen.

Is there something you would like to obtain that you have not as yet received? Well, don't give up. *The Word of God shows you how to obtain the unobtainable.* The Bible is God's "how-to" book of success. The more I study the Word of God, the more convinced I am that success comes from spending time with Him, and in His Word. It will make you a success. Success can be defined in these ways: to hit the mark, to have a favorable outcome, to receive results hoped for, to have things turn out as planned, or to obtain a desired end.

There's a beautiful story about the man who made it possible for us to be in this country today. If he had not been raised up for a very specific cause, this might not now be the United States of America, but a very

different country. His name is Christopher Columbus.
Many things have been said about his Christian faith.
As we know, he set out to prove that the world was
round, not flat. A few scholars of that day believed the
world was round, but the common belief was that the
earth was flat. Based on his assumption, Columbus
sought a shorter trade route to the area we call Asia.
He sought a new course.

He had a plan, a purpose, and a goal. He wanted
to achieve something. He finally was granted by the
Queen of Spain the large amount of money needed to
support his trip. He obtained three ships and filled
them with provisions. Then he hired crews for the ships
and set sail.

He plotted his course. He said, "This is the direction I am going." He had a goal and a purpose. He
didn't say, "One ship will go this direction, another is
going that direction, and the third one another direction." He had a specific plan and a strong purpose. He
was single-minded. He was going to discover a new
route to the Indies, proving that the world is round.

The first several weeks of the trip were pleasant.
But as the trip was prolonged, the men became more
restless. They began to go by what they saw. They
began to experience storms at sea. They began to fear
the things that came upon them. They began to be led
by the dictates of their senses. They knew they were
in unknown waters and even feared falling off the edge
of the flat earth.

But Christopher Columbus had faith in God. He
prayed three or four times a day and then told his men,
"The Lord will see us through." Several times the wind
was still, and they were becalmed. The ships went

nowhere; they just sat there in the heat. And the crew cried out. The men wanted to take over the ship. They wanted to mutiny. They wanted to dissolve his plan and stop trying to reach his goal. They wanted to be failures. But Christopher Columbus wanted to be a success. He said, "God will see us through."

In one last attempt at mutiny, his men surrounded him and rose up against him. They wanted to take over the ships and turn back. The Greater One swelled big inside of Columbus, and he said, "Sail on! Sail on!" He knew something they didn't know. He was about to obtain something that up until then had been unobtainable. But he had the inspiration of the Spirit of God. He had faith to persevere. He had the faith to go on.

Success is defined as hitting the mark, obtaining a desired end, having a favorable outcome, receiving results hoped for, or having things turn out as planned. Of course, it turned out right for Christopher Columbus. He achieved the success he had hoped for and far greater than he knew to think or ask for. He succeeded because he had the corresponding actions of faith to continue sailing on.

Jesus has come to rescue us from failure and to restore us to success. Again, I refer to Joshua 1:8 — God's formula for success.

> This book of the law shall not depart out of thy mouth; but thou shalt meditate therein day and night, that thou mayest observe to do according to all that is written therein: for then thou shalt make thy way prosperous, and then thou shalt have good success.

Keep God's Word in your mouth. God's Word shall not depart from your mouth. Keep on saying what God says and speak the Word only. To *meditate* means "to ponder and think upon and study." Meditating on

God's Word gives you understanding of how you can make your way prosperous. Meditating will give you understanding of how to do the will of God, which is the Word of God in your life. Meditating and spending time in God's Word gives you understanding of what to do to be successful in life. Then you will make your way prosperous and have success.

I want to point out something to you: **This book of the law shall not depart out of thy mouth; but *thou* shalt meditate. . ...** Who is the *thou* God is speaking about? You are *thou*. Read on: **That *thou* mayest observe to do according to all that is written therein: for then *thou* shalt make thy way prosperous, and then *thou* shalt have good success.** God told Joshua *you* four times.

You determine your level of success. You make the choice. God has made His choice. He sent the substance of things hoped for, which is faith. Now He has placed the ball in your court. It's your move. You determine the level of achievement and your level of success. The choice is yours. You choose. There is a saying, "Not to choose is to choose." You decide, even if your decision is not to decide and not strive and not try anything.

Joshua 1:8 tells us you will make your way prosperous. When? After you get information and add meditation and application. The choice is yours. Just how much to you want to achieve? Do you want to be a 30-fold, a 60-fold, or a 100-fold Christian? If you really believe you are a God-kind of creature, then the success of God and the things of God will begin to work in your life.

Many things are said in God's Word about doing the things of God. Ephesians 3:20 says, **Now unto him that is able to do exceeding abundantly above all that we ask or think, according to the power that worketh in us.** What God does in and through you is relative to, or according to, the power that is operative in you. This verse might be clearer to you if we reverse the two phrases in it. This is a proper paraphrase of this scripture:

According to the amount of power that works in us, God is able to do exceeding abundantly above all that we think.

Let me give you an example of how God will work exceeding abundantly in our behalf. We were leasing the parking lot around our church building, then we decided to buy it. The contract was drawn up but, suddenly, the deal fell through. And I had asked God for parking. I wasn't specific in saying "this lot" or "that lot." But I had asked God for parking. I didn't care which lot it was. That very day, some people came to see us and said, "We want to make you a deal you can't refuse."

They made us a much better offer than the first one — an offer which suited us perfectly. You see, God had something much better for us. God was able to do **exceeding abundantly above all that we** (could) **ask or think.** And He did it **according to the power that worketh in us** (or was operative in us). God provided property which is now worth several times more than we paid for it. It's worth millions.

I lean heavily on being a doer of God's Word. We've had various ministers come here and try to figure out what we're doing that is resulting in so much success.

The majority of them say that we emphasize strongly the corresponding actions of faith. And I believe that.

Applied Faith Is Applied Power

Applying and releasing the power of God in your life also can be called corresponding actions of faith.

Keep therefore the words of this covenant, and do them, that ye may prosper in all that ye do.
                    Deuteronomy 29:9

In this scripture, also, we find that keeping God's Words causes us to prosper. Acting on God's Word is applied power. Applied faith is applied power. When you begin to act on God's Word, you're releasing the ability of God to work in your behalf.

But whosoever looketh into the perfect law of liberty (God's Word), **and continueth therein, he being not a forgetful hearer, but a doer of the work, this man shall be blessed in his deed** (corresponding actions of faith).

                    James 1:25

This verse says that whoever continually looks into God's Word shall be blessed in his deeds — his corresponding actions. Who is so blessed? Whoever looks. Whoever sees himself as God sees him. Whoever sees himself as more than a conqueror. Whoever sees himself identified with Christ in His death, burial, and resurrection, and seated with him in a position of authority. Whoever sees himself healed by the stripes of Jesus. Whoever sees himself prospering. Whoever sees himself as a success. This man shall be blessed in his deed! Who? The man who looks into the perfect law of liberty.

God's Word regulates you for success. It lines you up and keeps you on the straight and narrow. You determine your level of success by the amount of effort you apply by seeing yourself and acting as God's Word says you are. Acting on the Word regulates your life for success.

> Now faith is the substance of things hoped for, the evidence of things not seen.
>
> For by it the elders obtained a good report.
>
> Through faith we understand that the worlds were framed by the word of God, so that things which are seen were not made of things which do appear.
>
> **Hebrews 11:1-3**

Faith is always in the present tense. It is now. Now faith is. What is it? It is the substance of things hoped for, the evidence of things not seen. The word *substance* can mean "something that causes things to stand." *Sub* means "below, an undercurrent, or an underlying factor that causes things to stand up." Does your faith cause you to be able to stand?

Faith is the substance or the underlying element or ingredient that causes you to be able to stand — not only to go forth advancing the Kingdom of God but also to be able to resist the onslaughts of the devil. Now faith is the substance or the real content of things.

Solid objects are made of atoms with protons and neutrons and other particles. But behind that physical substance is the real supernatural substance, the real content, that causes us to stand. That is the Word of God, the substance known as faith. Faith is the true content of everything. God even spoke you into existence. God used His words of faith, and you are here by faith.

By faith we understand that the worlds [during the successive ages] were framed — fashioned, put in order and equipped for their intended purpose — *by* the word of God, so that what we see was not made out of things which are visible.

Hebrews 11:3 AMP

The worlds were brought into existence, formulated, structured, and given content by the Word of faith. Faith is the supernatural content of everything. Now faith is the substance, or the real content, of things hoped for. Hope is in the mental realm. You express your will, your desires, your aims, and your goals in life. God said we are to delight in Him and in His Word and, as we do, He will give us the desires of our heart.

Delight thyself also in the Lord; and he shall give thee the desires of thine heart.

Psalm 37:4

Your desires are the finished product of the things you hoped for. They are the things you would like to see come to pass. Delight yourself in the true root, the true foundation, the true content of all success — the Word of God. Then God will give you success. He will give the desires, the finished product of the things you hoped for.

I get excited thinking about faith, the substance of things hoped for. God didn't just land a house on the earth for man to live in. He put the raw materials here for man to build houses and buildings and highways and automobiles. God didn't create the earth with buildings and cars. He put in your heart the spiritual substance that gives you the ability to get those things. He gave you the measure of faith, or the substance of anything you could hope for within His will. (Rom. 12:3.)

God goes one better than giving you a fish to eat. He shows you how to fish. God did better than giving you a house. He gave you the materials to build a house with. Do you see that? God went a step farther. He didn't just give you something. He gave you the source of it. He gave you the spiritual substance known as faith. And through that spiritual substance, you can achieve success in any endeavor that you put your hands to do if you'll substantiate it and back it up with God's Word.

Even in my thinking about cars and some all-time favorite years and models, God spoke to me. I wanted a 1965 Thunderbird, but I didn't have the faith to obtain it. God spoke to me and said, "I have given you the substance to be able to obtain anything. I have given you faith which can obtain!"

Faith will get you into right-standing with God. It will bring you into a position that the flesh will strive for years to obtain, but the flesh can't get you into a position of being right with God. The Spirit of God can, though. Faith can cause you to appropriate the shed blood of Jesus Christ at Calvary so that you can be in right-standing with the Creator of the world, and faith can cause you to believe that you are in right-standing with God. Faith will get you healed. Faith will cause the blessings of God and the benefits of Calvary to be released in your life.

Faith Is a Spiritual Ingredient

Faith is the raw material of everything that is seen and not seen. Faith is the substance, the ingredient, the content, the supporting factor of everything that is seen. By faith we stand. The worlds were formulated and brought into existence by the Word of God.

A seed can be defined as "something pre-programmed to be played back at a later day." God has given you that ingredient, faith, as a seed. You have been given in seed form the ingredient or the substance of everything. You must receive it and allow it to grow and develop in you. You determine your level of success. The Bible is God's book of success. Let's play it back loud and clear.

> This book of the law shall not depart from thy mouth; but thou shalt meditate therein day and night, that thou mayest observe to do according to all that is written therein: for then thou shalt make thy way prosperous, and then thou shalt have good success.
> Joshua 1:8

Observe to do. You will understand how to make your way prosperous and deal wisely in all of the affairs of life. You will have good success.

> Now faith is the substance of things hoped for, the evidence of things not seen.
>
> For by it the elders obtained a good report.
> Hebrews 11:1,2

What was the good report? It was the promises of God obtained by faith. Confessions of faith bring into reality the good report. Look at these examples of obtaining by faith:

> By faith Abel (v. 4).
>
> By faith Enoch (v. 5).
>
> By faith Noah (v. 7).
>
> By faith Abraham (v. 8).
>
> Through faith also Sara herself received strength to conceive seed, and was delivered of a child when she was past age, because she judged him faithful who had promised.
> Hebrews 11:11

Sarah received strength to obtain that which was unobtainable. She and Abraham were past the age of childbearing and couldn't have children when they were young. Naturally speaking, it was impossible for them to have a child. But through that spiritual ingredient known as faith — the true content of everything — Sarah had strength and power and force to conceive. She obtained a good report. The good report was that little Isaac had been born.

Sarah means "mother of many." *Abraham* means "father of many." God gave them those names. God called them father and mother of countless multitudes. God promised them offspring. Through faith in God's promise, Sarah received strength to conceive. Faith obtained that good report, that good confession. Confessions of faith obtain and bring into reality the good reports. *To obtain* means "to get possession of by effort." Faith without corresponding actions is dead, inoperative, incomplete. But faith with works becomes perfected or fully matured. It blossoms into reality. Faith with action causes things hoped for to become reality.

Faith is power. Hebrews 11:11 says Sarah **received strength to conceive seed.** Faith gave Sarah strength. Faith caused Sarah to be strong. *Strong* means "able." Faith made Sarah able in her physical body to conceive. *Strength* also means "soundness and ability to carry out wishes." *Strength* means "power." Sarah had the power to receive strength. Power can be used actively. Once again, faith can be known as a spiritual power.

Faith can be used in two ways. It can be used actively to subdue and to advance and to receive. Faith can also be used to stand and resist the devil and to restore the things taken away in works of the devil. Faith can be used to advance or to stand and resist the onslaughts of Satan.

Faith gave Sarah strength and power to obtain what was unobtainable. And God has given you the measure of faith. You determine your level of success, not corporately as a giant body, but individually. It doesn't matter who you are or where you come from. As a believer, you have the power of choice. You must decide. You make your way prosperous with God's Word.

Faith Without Works Will Not Work

Works means "acting on what is believed." It simply means corresponding actions of faith.

> **Even so faith, if it hath not works, is dead, being alone.**
>
> **. . . I will shew thee my faith by my works.**
>
> **For as the body without the spirit is dead, so faith without works is dead also.**
>
> **James 2:17,18,26**

An example of how you can make your way prosperous with God's Word is found in Mark 5:25. Remember the woman with the issue of blood? Here is a striking example of a woman who was sick and healing had been unobtainable.

> **And a certain woman, which had an issue of blood twelve years,**
>
> **And had suffered many things of many physicians, and had spent all that she had, and was nothing bettered, but rather grew worse.**
>
> **When she had heard of Jesus, came in the press behind, and touched his garment.**
>
> **Mark 5:25-27**

When she heard of Jesus (faith comes by hearing — Rom. 10:17), the author and finisher of our faith (Heb. 12:2), faith began to come. Spiritual strength began to arise in her when she heard of Jesus. When she heard the Word, strength began to rise up in her to obtain the unobtainable. When she heard of Jesus, she came in the press of the crowd behind and touched his garment.

First, she had information. She became informed. When you become informed, you become inspired. I'm sure she thought upon what Jesus said. For out of the abundance of her heart, out of the abundance of the spiritual substance known as faith, her mouth spoke. She began to speak, and she said this:

> For she kept saying, If I only touch His garments, I shall be restored to health.
>
> And immediately her (flow of) blood was dried up at the source, and (suddenly) she felt in her body that she was healed of her (distressing) ailment.
> **Mark 5:28,29** AMP

She was *informed*. She meditated. The Word of God was in her mouth, and she was not letting it depart. She *demonstrated* corresponding actions of faith. She had received the ingredient of things hoped for. She had the substance. She had the raw material of her healing. And when she began to act upon what she believed, she touched his garment, and faith with actions conceived, and the woman was healed.

Faith must work. You must put your faith to work. You must give it something to do. Faith is like a servant. Unless you give a servant something to do and feed him, he will not have the strength to do anything. He will become weak. You must give your faith something to do. Faith is an act, an action, a work. It has to be put to work before it can become activated and operative and give substance to things hoped for. Not foolishness at work, but faith at work.

Faith comes through God's Word. You put the Word to work. You work the Word. The woman of Mark 5 received as we must receive. She heard. Faith comes by hearing. Faith, the substance of healing, came. The substance of prosperity comes. A sound mind comes. Infilling of the Holy Spirit comes through the hearing of God's Word. You must hear the Word, believe the Word, speak the Word, and finally, act on the Word.

For she kept saying (v. 28). The Word of God was in her mouth. She acted. She pressed in and touched His garment. That is corresponding action of faith. The Bible speaks of those who look into the perfect law of liberty. She saw herself healed. She saw herself touching the hem of His garment. She saw herself being made whole. She saw herself acting on the Word of God.

The woman was looking into the perfect law of liberty and received liberty from the bondage of that sickness. She looked into the perfect law of liberty, and continued therein, and was blessed in her deeds. (James 1:25.) She was blessed in her actions of faith and received healing. She put her faith to work and received strength and power. Then she acted upon that power. It became applied faith and applied power in her life. And when she began to act upon the Word of God, she was made whole!

Recently, I ministered to a woman who had suffered terribly from arthritis and bursitis in her entire body for about 12 years. She'd been working on a radio telethon, and I was broadcasting from that station. She left the station and drove home listening to our broadcast. I began to speak the Word, and faith began to rise in her heart.

She had already heard my teaching series, "Harnessing the Human Mind," which includes testimonies of people receiving healing when they began to pull down strongholds and cast down imaginations. They began to see how to be single-minded, spiritually minded, and not double-minded. As she drove along, this woman said to herself, "If I can just get back to that radio station and get to Brother Tilton and have him pray the prayer of faith, God will heal me." Faith had given this woman strength. So she turned around and went back to the station.

She was like the woman in Mark 5 and also had suffered many things of many physicians. But when she heard the truth, faith came. She came into the station and began to pace back and forth outside my studio. I could see her outside the window, pacing and looking in at me. Finally, she talked someone into coming into the studio with a message: "Brother Tilton, there is a woman here who desperately needs you to pray for her."

Just before she came in, I had been relating a testimony. Under the inspiration of the Holy Spirit and unplanned, I had related a testimony of how a woman was healed through a supernatural miracle. So when this woman came into the studio, she said, "Brother Tilton, I have suffered for years, but I have faith that when you pray the prayer of faith for me, God will heal me. I heard you on the radio while driving home, and I knew if I could just get back here and have you pray the prayer of faith, I would be healed."

I prayed for her, bound the powers of darkness, and spoke healing into her body. And God gloriously healed her right there in the radio station studio! Now, why did God heal her? Faith is an act. She received faith from hearing the Word, then she acted on her faith in returning to be prayed for. Finally, she took the final step. She received God's power for healing.

God is no respecter of persons. The Word is no respecter of persons. Faith is no respecter of persons. Some folks think that God may heal them sometimes and that sometimes He may not. But that thought is not scriptural. There are times when God heals someone without an ounce of faith. That's called mercy. That is called grace. Why does He do it? I don't know. Someday I'll ask Him. But I can guarantee this: He always will heal on faith. He always heals someone acting on the Word and releasing the power of God in his life.

God will heal all the time by faith. Only occasionally does He heal people sovereignly. He always will heal when you act on faith, not belief or mental assent, but real faith — 100 percent of the time! God has given you the substance of faith, the substance of healing, the substance of prosperity. He has given you the ingredients to receive the desired results: hopes becoming reality, dreams being fulfilled, giving you the desires of your heart. It's your move. That woman acted on the Word. She gave her faith something to do. She put it to work.

Not long ago, we were ministering in Denison, Texas. Many people were born again, faith was high, and the word of knowledge began to operate through me. God told me someone there had problems in her head like a migraine headache, but it wasn't a migraine. Her symptoms were unusual and strange. I asked who that was.

A lady came forward with a scarf partially covering her face. She had been suffering for about 20 years from a very painful disease. It's supposed to be one of the most painful things anyone can be attacked with. She was so sensitive to pain that any pressure at all, even the wind, would cause unbearable pain. She had to wear a scarf everywhere she went, inside or outside.

She came up to me and said, "Brother Tilton, I live in Denison, and I listen to you on the radio every day. I know you are a busy man and hard to see. But I told the Lord that if He would just make a way so that I could have you pray for me, I know I'll be healed. God has answered my prayer. When I heard you were coming to Denison, I knew I had to get here. I knew God would heal me."

Now I know that it's not me but the prayer of faith that heals the sick. Not a prayer of doubt and disbelief, not hope so, not cross your fingers, not rub a rabbit's foot and hope and pray, but the prayer of faith. Faith is an act. And I knew God would heal her with talk like that. In a moment of time, those powers of darkness were broken. The anointing of God and the prayer of faith saved the sick. The Lord raised that woman up. She took the scarf off and began to feel of her face. There was no pain in her body anywhere. She was so happy! You would be too, if you had just gotten healed of one of the most painful diseases known to man, tic douloureux.

Remember that beautiful passage in John 5 about a man who had suffered from an infirmity for 38 years? He was waiting by the pool of Bethesda. At a certain season, an angel of the Lord would trouble the waters and the first person to get in the water would be healed. But this man didn't have the strength or power to get into the waters by himself. He was lame, and he had no one to help him into the pool.

Then Jesus walked by. Jesus, the author and the developer of faith, walked by. Faith, the Word of Faith, walked by. Jesus said to this lame man, **Wilt thou be made whole?** (John 5:6). Faith was there to give him strength to obtain what had been unobtainable for 38 years. When Jesus walked into the scene, the unobtainable became obtainable. When Jesus came on the scene, the man's faith was developed.

Then Jesus said, **Rise, take up thy bed, and walk** (John 5:8). He asked the man if he wanted to be healed. He gave the Word that would heal him. The man chose. He chose change. He chose help. He chose Jesus. He chose healing. **Wilt thou be made whole?** (v. 6). You also choose. The man had to choose to put his faith to work. Jesus already had made the choice to heal him, and the next step was up to the man. Jesus was saying, "Are you going to receive what I have to give you? Are you going to act in faith?"

What happened next? The man put his faith to work: **And immediately the man was made whole, and took up his bed, and walked** (John 5:9). Jesus didn't reach down and drag him up. He made the man make the next move. Suddenly, faith was there to give the man strength. He was able to obtain what had been unobtainable for 38 years.

The next move is yours. You have to decide your level of success. You have to decide what you're going to receive. You have to decide what is going to be converted from spiritual substance into reality in your life. Faith with works causes faith to reach its supreme expression.

4
PLANNING PUT INTO ACTION

This chapter deals with wise planning and how to have correct planning in whatever you're doing for God. Of course, we base our teaching on scriptural aspects of God's laws for success. And God's book, the Bible, is God's book of success. A law is something that regulates and rules and guides. And God's Word guides and regulates your life for success.

I'm glad that I am allowing the Word of God to regulate my life for success. It works every time. No matter how hard the storms blow and the winds may beat vehemently against your house, if it is founded and established upon the rock, it will not fall. That rock is hearing, then doing, the Word of God. God's Word will regulate your life for success. Say this aloud, so you can hear it in your own voice:

"God's Word is regulating my life for success. That means I hit the mark. I attain desired ends. Things hoped for come to pass because the Word is regulating my life."

We've learned some secrets from God's Word concerning wise planning. Because of that, new goals and vistas are continually opening up to us. In Matthew 6:34 our Lord says, **Take therefore no thought for the morrow.** Many times, people think that verse means they should not plan for the future. Consequently, their lives are a little bit confused. But Jesus was talking about having anxious concern, worrying and fretting about the things which tomorrow will bring.

There's nothing wrong with wise planning. The ant plans for the winter and stores up accordingly. We are told to consider her ways and be wise. (Prov. 6:6-8.) God's Word contains wisdom to help you prepare and plan for the things you're believing Him for. The Word of God plans. A man must build his house upon the rock or a good foundation. That foundation is knowing and acting upon God's Word.

Of course, *there is more than just saying the words.* It means to have understanding of that Word. Faith does not come until you understand a promise from God's Word. The seed is not sown until you understand a promise from God's Word. Faith does come by hearing. **Therefore whosoever heareth these sayings of mine, and doeth them** — he who hears these sayings and understands them — will have faith come (Matt. 7:24).

It's important for you to understand this. Faith does not come — the seed is not sown in your heart — until you understand a promise from God's Word. Faith comes by hearing and understanding what was heard. Let's look at Proverbs 24 as it is paraphrased in *The Living Bible*:

> **Any enterprise is built by wise planning, becomes strong through common sense, and profits wonderfully by keeping abreast of the facts.**
>
> **Proverbs 24:3,4** TLB

The word *enterprise* means "any undertaking, project, or business venture." Any enterprise must first of all begin with wise planning. God wants you to have the wisdom and prudence to successfully manage your home and business. God wants you to develop in business, and learn to correctly develop and manage your household. God is raising up His people to be *paymasters for the gospel* in these last days.

God doesn't want you to be ignorant. He doesn't want you to be foolish. He wants you to have wisdom and prudence. Wisdom comes with riches and honor in her left hand and length of days in her right. (Prov. 3:16.) So seek wisdom, for these other blessings come with the package.

Sometimes I see ministries which do not follow good business management and, somewhere down the line, they have problems and do strange things trying to raise money. They end up in debt and about to close down. Many of these problems stem from ignorance, not because the devil is stealing their money. It was just plain old ignorance or darkness on their part. They missed it when it came to wise planning. Any enterprise, undertaking, or project must come with wise planning.

The scripture goes on to say that any enterprise built on wise planning, or wisdom, becomes strong through common sense. Some people seem to think there's no such thing as common sense in the faith teaching. They think common sense was done away with, but that's not true. Basically common sense is prudence. Wisdom says, **I wisdom dwell with prudence** (Prov. 8:12). Those are two different types of wisdom. Use prudence or common sense when developing an enterprise or a business venture.

. . . Becomes strong through common sense, and profits wonderfully by keeping abreast of the facts. A profit is a return on your investment. When you invest time in the Word of God, you receive a profit.

As with architects, Christians need to spend time in planning. The men working on our new church building had to plan, or they wouldn't have known how to build it. Such things don't just happen. There is nothing wrong with having some good plans. We profit wonderfully. We have a return on our investment. We have invested money into those plans. We have invested money and time planning out how we're going to build things. In the beginning stages, as with a new church building, you don't see much. But planning had to take place before you could see anything. It takes a season, a period of time for something to develop and grow up. The reward of planning will show up when you start the building construction.

Ecclesiastes speaks of seed time and harvest — a time to sow, a time to reap.

> To every thing there is a season, and time to every purpose under the heaven:
>
> A time to be born, and a time to die; a time to plant, and a time to pluck up that which is planted.
> **Ecclesiastes 3:1,2**

The farmer first has to choose the kind of seed he wants to sow, based upon what type of return he wants. He gets the seed, then waits until the soil and the weather and the timing are just right. Then he sows that seed. But between the time he sows and the time he reaps is a season. Everything has a season. In everything we endeavor to do, there is a period of time before it fully develops and matures into reality.

Any enterprise, undertaking, project, or business venture is built by wise and prudent planning and wisdom. Then it becomes strong through common sense and prudence and profits wonderfully by keeping abreast of the facts. We need to learn about three areas: *planning, common sense, and keeping abreast of the facts.*

Wise Planning Is Common Sense

Wise planning involves budgeting how much to spend each month. Wise planning *is* common sense. Let's say you budget money for the month and then go to the grocery store. You walk through the junk food section and those package labels jump out and tell you, "Yummy in the tummy," and you blow the budget. That's not common sense. That's not prudent. From that error you can be in trouble at the end of the month when the bills come. Then you have to call on God to bail you out.

That's not God's best. He will bail you out, but that's not His best for you. Plan wisely, use common sense, have prudence, and keep abreast of the facts. That means keeping your checkbook tallied and keeping out of overdrafts.

Several years ago — due to not keeping abreast of the facts — we found that, in addition to our regular bills, we owed $53,000 in unexpected bills. We had kept abreast of the facts to a certain extent, but details we'd neglected really showed up. So we hadn't kept abreast of the facts as we should have. We had to get over into the area of mercy and grace with our faith — and God's grace was sufficient. But we wouldn't have been forced to go through some of those things if we had done more wise planning. Let me tell you what we did to get out of that one.

We played Kenneth Hagin's tape about *El Shaddai*, the God of Plenty, day and night until we were saturated with the Word of God. We stacked up all the bills which had piled up. All our employees had those tapes, and all of us played them day and night to ourselves and to those bills. We released our faith and money began to come in from all directions.

We paid the bills. But the way we had to go about getting those bills paid was not God's best way. That's the way a child operates. In order to be good stewards and handle large sums of money for the gospel, we must be sharp, responsible believers. If you confess that God is raising you up to be a good paymaster, operating in the ministry of giving, with thousands of dollars flowing through your hands into the gospel, then you must be a good steward. Good stewardship is your corresponding action of faith.

You must be a responsible person. And the best place to begin is with your own checkbook at home and your own budget. Marte and I believe that. We practice it. We pay our bills. We have perfect credit. Years ago, if we needed dollars, we went out and did something to earn dollars. Even if we had to do something we didn't like to do, we did it to pay our bills. I believe that's the way all believers should be. I believe you need to be responsible.

Some say that preachers are among the worst credit risks. That is a disgrace on the ministry. That's not the way God would have it. I want those bankers and financiers out in the world to be eager to do business with believers. I want them to say, "They are the ones with integrity of heart. They keep their word." We can just call our banker and get another car loan. He only asks the bottom line figure, the serial number, and the make of car. But that came about because we were responsible people, having integrity of heart, and doing what we said we were going to do.

If you make a pledge, you need to keep that pledge. It builds character. It builds and develops the nature of God in your life. Use wise planning and common sense. You profit wonderfully by keeping abreast of the facts. Be faithful in small things. Learn to be responsible. Become a person of integrity. When you give your word, keep it. Keeping your word builds character. It builds and develops the nature of God in your life.

The thoughts of the diligent tend only to plenteousness (Prov. 21:5). If you are a good steward over what God has given you, He will bless you and give you more. I believe with all of my heart that God blesses a busy person. I believe we need to be busy doing the things of God, then God will bless us more.

We have taught Bible school students here and in other parts of the world. I've told them that if they go out and be busy and faithful with whatever their hands find to do, God will bless them, and they will end up in their proper ministry work.

I didn't wait for people to call me up and invite me to preach. I couldn't find any scripture that spoke of waiting for someone to call me up and ask me to go preach in his church. The Bible says this:

> **And he** (Jesus) **said unto them, Go ye into all the world, and preach the gospel to every creature.**
> **Mark 16:15**

Luke 10:7 tells us **the labourer is worthy of his hire**. The Lord told those He sent out to go into a city and, if they were received, to let their peace rest upon it. If they were not received, He told them to go on to the next city. And that's the way we went out. We continually stayed busy, feeding the people, and preaching the gospel to anyone we could find. We didn't wait for someone to call us up. We were diligent. We went out and acted upon the Word of God. And the Word of God maintained us. Many times, we didn't have meetings. Each time, the Spirit of God dealt with our hearts.

Your re-born spirit man can be developed to such an extent that you can hear from God exactly what He wants you to do. This is intuition. This is conscience, the inner voice, the inner man talking to you. He will lead you and give you direction.

Several times, if we'd been hard-headed and not listening to others, we would've missed God by a long way. But we stayed sensitive before the Spirit of God, and we heard God. We did what God told us to do, and He maintained and blessed us. We kept abreast of the facts. We were diligent. And God continued to bless us.

That's the way we came to Dallas. We didn't wait for someone to call us. God sent us to Farmers Branch, a suburb of Dallas. We didn't wait for five committees to vote on whether or not they liked the way I preach or if they approved of my background. We stayed sensitive before the spirit of God and simply did what He told us to do. He blessed and sustained us when we got here. Now I have more speaking engagements than I know what to do with.

Our ministry wasn't always like that. But it developed because I simply taught the Word of God. Our ministry developed because we did what God said, instead of waiting on what man thought we ought to do. We were diligent in what our hands found to do. We checked our crops, too. And we still check our crops. We sow seeds into the different facets of our ministry.

I walk around nearly every morning to every facet of the ministry, even if it is just to walk through and let the Spirit of God radiate off of me or flow through me. I do this to allow the Spirit of God to deal with my heart and perceive any particular matters that may need a little extra encouragement. Sometime during the day, the Spirit of God may tell me something about a particular department or need or change. I write it down in my notebook or go to that department and tell them about it. My spirit man is trained to be disciplined and to be able to hear the voice of God.

We have determined to teach the Word of God and do what He says to do. As long as we continue to do that, we'll know success. Recently, there was a certain matter that came up in the offices, a way of smoothing out communication. God had told Marte a certain thing to do two days before, but she hadn't told me anything. The Spirit of God spoke to me clearly, and it was the same thing along business lines. I told Marte and, of course, she got excited because God had told each of us the same thing. It was a word of wisdom. I believe God blesses your efforts. Man plans his way, but God directs his steps. We had needed direction in some things we had planned. God was giving direction to our steps.

> In all thy ways acknowledge him, and he shall direct thy paths.
>
> Proverbs 3:6
>
> A man's heart deviseth his way: but the Lord directeth his step.
>
> Proverbs 16:9

To plan means "to think out a way of doing things and come up with a creative way of causing something to come to pass." It's a detailed method, thought out beforehand, like architectural drawings. *To plan* means "to design something which stresses the outcome."

Two Types of Wise Planning

This is a message for those who desire to be successful. This is a combination of practicality and wisdom. You know, there are two types of wisdom or wise planning. There is the *sophia* wisdom and the *phronesis* wisdom.

Sophia wisdom is the infinite, perfect comprehension of all that might be, insight into the true nature of everything. This is the theoretical side of wisdom. Some read the Bible and memorize it, but don't do anything with it. It's just theory to them. Of course, you must have the theoretical side before you can add the practical side. You must have information to be informed. Then you must use the information.

Phronesis wisdom is the practical side. It is the ability to discern modes of action. It is the "for every action there is a reaction" or "cause-and-effect" wisdom. This means ability to view the results of an action. *Phronesis* wisdom is prudence and common sense and good judgment. It sees cause and effect. It says, "If you do *this*, then *that* will happen."

For example, **"Show yourself friendly, and you will have friends."** The theory part, or *sophia* wisdom, would be to know and comprehend this principle based on Proverbs 18:24. The practical side, or *phronesis* wisdom, would be to actually go out and show yourself friendly. That shows understanding of cause and effect. First, have the overview of what causes people to respond, and then have the practical side of wisdom.

A merry heart doeth good like a medicine (Prov. 17:22) can be the practical side. Start laughing and being a happy person all the time, and it becomes like medicine being ministered to your spirit man. Of course, out of your heart flow the issues of life. Nothing is so serious that you can't laugh. I've had some opportunities for great stress on my life. And each time, I just go back into my office, shut the door, put my feet up on the desk, and laugh. Or, I may invite someone to go out with me for a snack and a few laughs. **He that is of a merry heart hath a continual feast** (Prov. 15:15).

With all the pressure in our ministry, if we didn't know how to escape it and operate in the Word, we wouldn't last very long. Any enterprise can be built on wise planning and can become strong through common sense. Sometimes businesses fail because people don't keep abreast of all the facts.

We've had to plan ahead for the expansion of our ministry. For example, we once rented a shopping center with 20,000 square feet of space, although we didn't have anything to put in it for awhile. But, soon, it was full and running over. It houses the mail department, tape production, the counseling center, and video theater. We used *sophia* wisdom, then *phronesis* wisdom. We only had it when we needed it because of wise advance planning, then acting on that plan. Without planning, we would sink.

Aren't you glad that any enterprise can be built on wise planning? Any enterprise can be strong through common sense and can profit wonderfully through keeping abreast of the facts.

Sometimes businesses fail because people don't keep abreast of the facts. Your household can fail, if you don't keep abreast of the facts. You must have a financial plan. If you're not wise in some of your purchases and in your credit card use, you can get into trouble. That is not God's best for your life. God didn't want you to get into that trouble to begin with. But His wisdom can get you out and keep you out.

Why is that some people plan and others don't? Some are just smarter than others. If you have blown it a few times, don't get angry at me, and don't get under condemnation. That's why you're studying this — to get smarter. You are smart for just studying this, so there's hope for you. Plan wisely. Watch what you're doing. Your income may not justify a certain purchase, so you need to believe God for more income before you make the purchase. Then you won't get into trouble at the end of the line. I know this is nuts-and-bolts stuff, but many people miss practical application.

Certain unavoidable situations do occur. But most times when people don't have enough money, it's because they have missed it. We don't want to miss God's best way. I don't want you to, and you don't want to. We want to learn to operate in prudence and good common sense. There's nothing wrong with common sense. **I wisdom dwell with prudence** (Prov. 8:12). That is the overview of things — the big picture (*sophia*) which works with cause and effect (*phronesis*).

Your recreated spirit will produce whatever you program into it — good, bad, or indifferent. You can plan something and, if it's in agreement with the Word of God and believable, your spirit man will attract the things necessary for success. And God will cause those things to come to pass in your life. God has given us the raw material to bring things into existence. That raw material is the spiritual substance known as faith.

I keep with me a notebook which has proven very beneficial in my planning. In it, I have written a list of people whom I wish to see. There also is a section for telephone numbers, a calendar, and a section on ideas. Then there is one section for each facet of our ministry: the church, Bible school, satellite division, radio and television, the *Arrow* newspaper, the Christian Academy, and others.

This notebook is for planning, a way of keeping abreast of the facts. As God gives me inspired thoughts on each of these areas of ministry, I write them down. I know the Creator is inside me. Christ, the Anointed One, the anointing is within me, and I continually confess that He gives me inspired thoughts.

Inspired thoughts on this verse got us to Dallas:

> **Roll your works upon the Lord — commit and trust them wholly to Him; [He will cause your thoughts to become agreeable to His will, and] so shall your plans be established and succeed.**
>
> **Proverbs 16:3** AMP

Roll upon the Lord your plan, your works, your detailed method of getting something done. He will cause your thoughts to be in agreement with His will and you shall succeed. When God gives you these thoughts, you need to write them down. Capture them before they escape your memory. How many times has God told you something or given you a revelation of a scripture and, because you didn't write it down, you lost it? If you had written it down, you could have gone back to it, looked at it, fed upon it, and pondered it in your heart.

God told people to write things down. In the Old Testament, people wrote scriptures on doorposts and wore phylacteries on their forehead and arms. Originally, a petition was a formal, written request. Make your petitions — your prayer requests — to God. How many times do you write down what you pray for? You should. Then you can scratch off each request as God answers. Seeing a page full of items scratched off is a powerful reminder to you of God's willingness to answer prayer.

The Vision Is the Seed

When we first moved to Farmers Branch, I wrote out my goals and the things I wanted to believe God for. I wrote out the different ways we were going to reach people. For one of our board of directors meetings, I drew a tree with a little seed and wrote *Word of Faith Concepts: Opportunities for Eternity.* That little seed was our vision. The little seed was the vision for Word of Faith that God had implanted into our hearts. That was the inspired thought and the vision.

> *The seed is the vision.*
>
> *The roots are the goals.*
>
> *The trunk is the planning.*
>
> *The branches are the priorities.*
>
> *The leaves are the corresponding actions.*
>
> *The fruit is the end result.*

When the seed — the vision — begins to grow, it puts down roots which are the goals, the things you want to accomplish. As a plant begins to grow, it develops a trunk which is your planning. In order to take the vision to the goal, there must be planning.

I wrote goals for our ministry in three areas: local, national, and international. The local goals included our home church and the ways we can reach people in the community. National goals include the radio and television ministries. The international goals have been centered around our plans for Bible colleges.

Regularly seeing and looking at those thoughts which I took time to crystallize on paper helped strengthen the vision in my heart of what God had called us to do. Then it gave birth to what we called

"Campaign Headquarters," because an atmosphere like that of a political campaign headquarters began to develop. In political campaigns, everyone gets excited about their "man." We ought to be excited about "our man," the Son of Man, Jesus Christ. So I said, "This is the campaign headquarters for Christ — reaching the city, state, nation, and world for Jesus." We have just begun to see the tree grow.

The branches are the priorities — the things needed to be done first in order to cause the goal to come to pass. And the leaves are the corresponding actions, based on priorities. Last comes a fully matured tree and the fruit that all started with a tiny seed!

We set our goals for a family church and Christian education center long before it came into manifestation. We committed this to prayer and believed it was what God wanted us to have. But it was two to three years before we had a Christian school and seminars for training the adults. Today, we have a K-12 Christian school, seminars, and training. We planned our media outreach before we ever went on radio or television. We also had planned our use of cassette tapes, books, videocassettes, and other related materials.

We had plans for our family church and for the pastor. There was a plan for Christian education — promoting mental and spiritual growth through the renewing of the mind — and a plan for entertainment.

In our offices, we prepared two giant boards. We spent days lining those boards and putting on them the 12 months of the year. We filled it in with names of those we believed God would send our way to minister to us in music and in the Word once a month. We actually did this more than a year in advance, because we practiced wise planning. We find we can get the best people to fit into our schedule when we have a plan. For some time, we've had guest speakers every three or four weeks. We control their spacing because we plan well in advance. Without that, we'd fail in seminar planning. We would be forced into others' schedules, taking whatever might be available. Instead of working us into their plans at the last minute, they work into our plans far ahead, which is good for us and for them. It helps them plan their schedules.

And God is blessing this system because it is wise planning. We use a detailed method with a design and structure. God has given us the raw materials, and He gives us the fulfillment, achievement, and enjoyment of seeing it come to pass. The plan began to work, the leaves came forth, and now the tree is bearing fruit.

All these things didn't just happen by chance. Our congregation didn't just accidentally show up. God gave us the raw material to work with, then blessed us as we put our hands to the plow. The same thing can happen in your family and church and business. Marte and I enjoy believing God for our marriage, home, and family. He has answered our prayers in ways that would astound you. We have committed things unto the Lord.

> A man's heart deviseth his way: but the Lord directeth his steps.
>
> Proverbs 16:9

> Let the Lord be magnified, which hath pleasure in the prosperity of his servant.
>
> Psalm 35:27

> Delight thyself also in the Lord; and he shall give thee the desires of thine heart.
>
> Psalm 37:4

He will cause the desires of your heart to come to pass. That is called the abundant life. It's more than just trudging along mumbling, "One of these days, I'll barely make it in!" I'm going to march in with my head held high. I've run the course. I have pressed toward the mark of the prize of the high calling. I have finished the course! It feels good to finish the course.

Remember how good you felt when you graduated from high school or when you finished a project on which you had worked for a long time? It feels great to reach your goal, doesn't it? Well, it's the same way with the things of God in this life, right now. I love to see God give us plans.

On our early plan, we had a board of directors and an advisory board. We had our ministry all mapped out with directors over each department reporting to me. We still have written goals and procedures for facets of our ministry. For example, we have written goals and procedures for prospects and methods of prospecting. I believe people need what we have here. So I gladly prospect for people. I'm a fisherman. Jesus spoke to my heart out loud and told me He would make me *a fisher of men.* And there is an anointing on me to catch men. I have fished for you.

Many people get born again at our church. That doesn't happen by chance. We are to be wise, and the Bible says that he who is wise will be winning souls. (Prov. 11:30.) You don't see a fisherman saying, "Today I'm going to catch some fish," and then going out into the middle of the lake swimming and wondering why he didn't catch any fish. He had no fishing equipment, no bait or lures. We have to lure people to what we have.

We should just think about fishermen. Some of them really catch a lot of fish. Why do some catch more than others? Because they use more wisdom. They go to the right place at the right time with the right bait and equipment. They exercise persistence and patience. We had plans for advertising, including the *Arrow* newspaper. We had bumper stickers, newspaper ads, radio spots, billboards, and radio and television programs.

We knew television would be a major national ministry for us. So our auditorium was planned and designed with television in mind before it ever was built. We constantly check ahead on equipment needs for television broadcasting. This does not all "just happen." We make many decisions in this manner: We look at our goals and see if the new opportunity fits into them. We don't stumble around and allow procrastination or the devil to steal opportunities which come along. If they fit into our vision, if the timing is right, and if the finances are there, then we do it. We use wise planning.

Here is a really different and unusual story of a man who followed God's principles of having a vision, of planning, and of carrying out that plan with persistence and patience. This man was 15 years old in 1940. He saw people around him doing just about nothing. And he made a written list of 127 things he wanted to do during his life.

He wanted to explore these rivers: the Nile, Amazon, Congo, Colorado, Yangtze, Niger, Orinoco in Venezuela, and Rio Coco in Nicaragua.

He wanted to study primitive cultures in the Congo, New Guinea, Brazil, Borneo, Sudan, Australia, Kenya, the Philippines, Ethiopia, Nigeria, and Alaska.

He wanted to climb Mount Everest, Kilimanjaro, McKinley, Kenya, Fuji, the Grand Tetons, and others.

He wanted to photograph Victoria Falls, Sutherland Falls, Yosemite Falls, and Niagara Falls.

He wanted to explore underwater coral reefs in Florida, the Great Barrier Reef in Australia, the Red Sea, the Fiji Islands, and the Bahamas.

He wanted to explore the Okeefenokee Swamp and the Everglades in Florida.

He wanted to visit the North and South Poles, the Great Wall of China, the Panama and Suez Canals, Easter Island, Vatican City, the Taj Mahal, the Eiffel Tower, the Blue Grotto, and the Tower of London.

He wanted to swim in Lake Victoria and Lake Superior. He wanted to skin dive to 40 feet, hold his breath two and one-half minutes underwater, and catch a 10-pound lobster.

He wanted to become an Eagle Scout, dive in a submarine, land and take off from an aircraft carrier, fly in a blimp, a balloon, a glider, and ride an elephant, a camel, an ostrich, and a bronco.

He wanted to go to church and to follow the John Muir Trail. He wanted to study native medicines and bring back useful ones.

He wanted to bag camera trophies of elephant, lion, rhino, cheetah, Cape buffalo, and the whale; to learn to fence; to teach a college course; to watch a cremation ceremony; to explore the depths of the sea; and to appear in a Tarzan movie.

He wanted to own a horse, a chimpanzee, a cheetah, and an ocelot. He wanted to build a telescope;

write a book and publish an article in *National Geographic*; high jump 5 feet, broad jump 15 feet, run a mile in five minutes, and perform 200 situps and 20 pullups.

He wanted to weigh 175 pounds; learn French, Spanish, and Arabic; read the entire Encyclopedia Britannica, the Bible from cover to cover, and the works of Shakespeare, Plato, Aristotle, Dickens, Thoreau, Hemingway, Twain, and others; and to become familiar with compositions of Bach and Beethoven, as well as to compose his own music.

He wanted to become proficient in the use of an airplane, a motorcycle, tractor, surfboard, rifle, pistol, canoe, microscope, football, basketball, bow and arrow, lariat, and boomerang.

He wanted to watch people walking on fire, milk a poisonous snake, light a match by shooting it with a .22 rifle, and learn to play polo.

He wanted to be a member of the Explorers Club and the Adventurers Club, to travel through the Grand Canyon on foot and in a boat, to go around the globe four times, and to visit the moon someday, if God willed.

He wanted to marry and have children and live to see the 21st century.

In November, 1940, this young man decided his life was not going to be mediocre and boring. He was going to do a few things in his life. There's no telling how long it took him to figure out what he was going to do. Perhaps he got all those goals from reading the encyclopedia.

In March of 1977, when he was 47 years old, he had completed 103 of his goals with 24 to go. He had five children and will be 70 when the year 2000 rolls around. And in 1977, he earned approximately $50,000 from his lectures about his adventures. He earned money from reaching his goals! If that man can do that much, how much should we Christians be able to do?

Jesus said unto him, If thou canst believe, all things are possible to him that believeth.

Mark 9:23

Jesus said that. He said it, and it is true for you and for me. Remember, any enterprise is built on wise planning. Reaching those 103 goals was the result of this man's planning when young. Your enterprise becomes strong through common sense and profits wonderfully by keeping abreast of the facts.

Let me give you seven steps which will help you accomplish your goals. I know some people who are working on this list, and they have doubled and tripled their income. They are living in divine health and enjoying freedom from all the curse of the law.

Seven Steps to Accomplish a Goal

1. *Take inventory of your life.* Find out where you are. What do you have in your possession that God can use? Galatians 6:7 says, **Whatsoever a man soweth, that shall he also reap.** Moses had a rod and David had a sling. Elijah used a meal barrel. But these possessions were nothing until the anointing of God came upon them.

2. *Become dissatisfied with second best.* You ought to look good, smell good, talk good, and live good. There is nothing like having on crisp, new clothes. Clothing is an extension of your personality. You may not like this message. You may not believe it. But I say God wants us to look like kings. We are as kings in this life.

We should be examples to the world of what God will do through His people. I believe God has the power to bless you greatly. If you will delight yourself in the Lord, He will give you the desires of your heart.

You say, "I'm not supposed to think about clothes." That's right. Once you think about the kingdom of God and seek it first, you'll end up with clothes. I give away ties and shoes and coats and am always getting those things given to me. It takes faith to receive new clothes. Proverbs 23:7 says, **As** (a man) **thinketh in his heart, so is he.** You will stop just drudging along when you stop seeing yourself drudging along. As a man thinks in his heart, so is he. There's nothing wrong with thinking like God thinks. God isn't poor. Jesus prayed, **Thy will be done in earth, as it is in heaven** (Matt. 6:10). The Bible says that in heaven the streets are pure gold. (Rev. 21:21.)

3. *Make up your mind what you are going to do.* Don't keep saying, "One of these days . . . . One of these days I'll go to Bible school. One of these days I'll read the Bible. One of these days, one of these days." Before people know it, they're old and that day never came because of procrastination and of never having made a decision. In John 5:6, Jesus asked, **Wilt thou be made whole?** Make decisions about what you're going to do with the Word of God in your life, and don't procrastinate.

4. *Have a plan.* Proverbs 16:3 says, **Roll your works upon the Lord** (AMP). The Apostle Paul had a plan. In Philippians 3:14, he said, **I press toward the mark for the prize of the high calling of God in Christ.**

5. *Stand on God's promises.* In Him, we live and move and have our being. Be a doer of the Word.

6. *Accept life and God's promises.* Start where you are. Don't start where someone else is. Start where you are — on your own faith, not someone else's. Where are you in your faith walk? You need to be believing God for small things before you tackle big things. Start where you are now. I'm sure you've said, "When I get to a certain point, I'll do that." Start doing "that" today, wherever you are, at the level you are.

Luke 16:16 says that we *press into* the kingdom of God. We must *press in* with our faith. Begin to walk in the promises of God's Word. They don't come easily. You receive them by faith, but you must begin to walk in them. And then they must be defended against the fowls of the air that would try to stop them from working in your life. Then you begin to grow and develop. As you walk in God's Word, you'll become stronger every day.

I've seen people come into our church when things were tough for them. Things weren't working out for them. But the Word of God began to smooth things out for them. They may have had to borrow a little money here and there, but now they are lending money. They have become the head and not the tail. (Deut. 28:13.)

I'll use our church as an example. We started from nowhere with nothing. We have doubled and redoubled. We grow in ministry and outreach from year to year. Every facet of our ministry grows and multiplies in size of outreach. And it's all to win souls, educate believers, and mobilize the army of God. This is not the normal mode of operation for American churches. But I believe it is the proper mode for the New Testament church in these last days. God is raising up super-churches, powerful churches.

For years, people thought we had to stay in small groups, not over 200. If we get to 250 members, we need to go across town and begin another church. Do you know what happened? The devil kept the churches small without the vision nor strength nor power to take over cities. When a church becomes big and strong, it becomes powerful. Get several thousand people gathering together, and they can do something big. They can take a city for Jesus.

More broadcast media need to be taken. More newspapers need to be taken. More radio stations need to be taken. And you don't do it with a handful of people. You do it with a large, unified body of believers who know what they are doing and where they are going and how to get there.

7. *Work your plan.* DO IT! DO IT! DO IT! Faith without works is dead. Work your plan. The anointing of God was behind David's sling when he killed the giant. The anointing of God was behind Moses' rod when he stretched it over the Red Sea to part the waters. The anointing of God was on the widow's meal barrel when Elijah said the barrel would not run dry or the oil fail in the cruse.

The anointing of God is behind a believer's life. It makes all the difference in the world. Instead of a minority, you become a majority! The world has yet to see how much God will do through a body of believers or an individual totally sold out and dedicated to the propagation of the gospel of the Lord Jesus Christ.

5
PERSEVERANCE AND PATIENCE

"Corresponding actions of inspired thoughts cause things hoped for to become reality." Several weeks ago, the Spirit of God said those words to me. As I meditated upon that, He spoke again and said, "Inspired thoughts are the Word of God."

The early apostles and disciples were moved upon by the inspiration of the Holy Spirit to write inspired thoughts — the New Testament. Corresponding actions of inspired thoughts — the Word of God — cause things hoped for to become reality.

We have gotten into several areas of God's laws for success. We have looked at applied faith or corresponding actions of faith. Faith is a spiritual substance. It is the ingredient, the substance, the undergirding that causes everything to stand. We understand that by faith the worlds were framed or structured by the Word of God.

A building is framed. The frame or structure of a building supports the whole building. We understand that through faith the worlds were framed or structured by the Word of God — *the word of faith*. This ingredient known as faith brings everything into existence. God gave us the raw material of everything. He gave us the spiritual substance known as faith. You have in your possession the raw material to possess the things hoped for.

There is an element which goes along with faith. That element is called patience. The Word of God is very plain about faith and patience. They're almost always linked together.

> Cast not away therefore your confidence, which hath great recompence of reward.
>
> For ye have need of patience, that, after ye have done the will of God, ye might receive the promise.
>   Hebrews 10:35,36

After ye have done the will of God (v. 36) is that time *after* you have taken the corresponding actions of faith. Then you receive and possess the promise. We're dealing with the subject of success. I have found that many believers and ministers don't understand how to continue and persevere in the things for which they are believing God. This is one of the greatest reasons for failure in the Body of Christ. Persevere until you receive the promise. Don't quit until you win.

If a farmer failed to persevere, he would never harvest a crop. He would have no crops to harvest, if he gave up and kicked his seed out of the soil. It's the same way with God's Word. It must be continually watered and you must exercise faith and patience. By continuing in the Word with faith and patience, whatever you are believing God for will come to maturity and bring forth a harvest of results.

God wants you to be a success! First of all, believe that God wants you to be a success. There are some things you can learn about success. I believe they are all available through the Spirit of God. I also believe we are all available to what the Spirit of God would teach us concerning success.

Patience and Persistence

I want to deal now with two primary words: *patience* and *persistence*. I analyze my life. I analyze the Word of God. I always want to know what causes me to be successful. Many times, people who have become successful lose that success or lose at least some portion of it, simply because they didn't know how they got it in the first place. But if you know how you obtained something, then you know how to get it again and how to keep it. That is only good common sense or prudence.

Now the word *patience* means "to sustain, to be steadfast, to endure, or to continue despite opposition." You must understand that there will be opposition in your walk with the Lord. First Peter says there is an adversary:

> **Be sober, be vigilant; because your adversary the devil, as a roaring lion, walketh about, seeking whom he may devour.**
>
> **1 Peter 5:8**

Your adversary opposes you and opposes the good in your life. He opposes anything you do which would cause you to become a success. He wants you to be a failure. He wants you to fail or to quit. He wants you to give up prematurely. There is a saying in the world, "Quitters never win, and winners never quit." The devil tries to get believers to quit continuing in the faith. He wants you to give up the faith. The Word of God is very clear in its instructions to the Church. Paul tells us, **Fight the good fight of faith, lay hold on eternal life** (1 Tim. 6:12).

We must continue doing the Word of God. We must continue to persevere. We must be persistent and exercise ourselves in patience. These two words, patience and persistence, go hand in hand. Basically, they have the same meaning. Persistence means "continuing in the faith in the face of opposition." It means "to endure." To have patience is to be steadfast and immovable, in spite of opposition. In other words, to persevere is to persist in what you're doing and have patience in it.

Two manifestations or fruit of your recreated spirit are longsuffering and temperance. (Gal. 5:22,23.) To be longsuffering (to have forbearance and patience) means "to be solid, firm, stable, and not to give up too soon." A believer who is stable is a believer with temperance. You should continue in the Word — continue being a doer of the Word, until you receive the promise.

A beautiful example of continuing to be a doer of the Word in spite of opposition is the way we faced our building program at Word of Faith World Outreach Center. We began this program almost the day we arrived. And I'm sure we will continue in a building program until Jesus returns.

If a plant is healthy, you'll have to continually change containers. You must re-pot a healthy plant from time to time, because it outgrows the container. A healthy congregation of believers is the same way. It will continually need a new sanctuary and facilities. We've had to constantly exercise our faith with patience in believing God for our sanctuary and its constant expansion and improvements. We had to purchase several properties for parking lots and expansion room. Each new purchase takes months, even years, to complete. It takes constantly fighting the good fight of faith to get those jobs done.

Some days, I start fighting a multi-headed dragon, and every head must be chopped off. Not one giant with one head, but it seems as if each giant, each project, has many heads and each has to be chopped off.

If I were a quitter, I would have quit long ago. But I understand how to persevere and how to stand.

Wherefore take unto you the whole armour of God, that ye may be able to withstand in the evil day, and, having done all, to stand.

Stand therefore . . . .

Ephesians 6:13,14

We've had plenty of opportunities to throw in the towel. But we have allowed longsuffering, forbearance, and temperance to operate in our lives. We didn't quit. We continued. Again, we've not succeeded by accident. Our work is planned out. We plan and foresee things. We see in advance that we'll need certain properties. We planned months ago for the successes of today. Months ago, we planned to take possession of land and goods that we are possessing today. We use continual planning with corresponding actions. This causes things to come into our possession.

Have you ever known someone who just gave up? Have you ever wanted to just give up? But don't give up! A quality that comes with a Christ-like life is that of not giving up, but continuing on — trusting and relying upon God. You must have confidence that the Word of God is operative and working in your life. Faith requires some hope to give substance to. So don't quit. Don't throw away your confidence.

Cast not away therefore your confidence, which hath great recompence of reward.

Hebrews 10:35

You could say having confidence in God and in the Word of God working in your life has compensation. Say this aloud so that you can hear yourself:

"The Word of God operative in my life has great compensation of reward. The Word of God and my acting upon it brings reward to me."

The above scripture in Hebrews continues: **For ye have need of patience** (Heb. 10:36). What does patience have to do with it? It keeps you from casting away your confidence. In other words, patience is a stabilizing factor in your continuing to do the Word of God. This force of patience comes in, undergirds your corresponding actions of faith, and keeps you acting on God's Word until you receive that compensation of reward. After you have done the will of God, your faith and patience are exercised by continuing to believe that you have received whatever you asked God for.

Several years ago, I talked to a Jewish man who was very precise in his business. He knew what he was doing. He was applying many truths out of God's Word. I asked this particular man if he had any words of wisdom for young men who were growing and prospering in business. I said, "If you were about to depart this world, and you wanted to leave some key to your success in your business, what would you say?"

He said, "Persistence, young man. Persistence. Continuing on in the face of all opposition."

Did you know that some people never attempt to do anything great for God for fear of what other people might think or say about them? If you are salty, you'll catch a little flack — you will catch some persecution. But if you can't handle a little persecution, you will probably never attempt anything big for God. You must have the faith to get out of the boat. We want to be able to overcome fear of criticism and fear of what other people might have to say about us.

Persistence means remaining immovable, remaining unchanged, or remaining fixed in a specified character position and condition. You should be fixed and continuing to do the Word believing that you've received the promise. There is a powerful force which can be released out of your spirit man. Once you get the power of God released out of your spirit man, keep that "faith switch" on. Then your faith can continue to work for you while you're possessing and receiving the promise.

Everything we have begun at Word of Faith World Outreach Center has taken much patience. It takes patience every day. I'm just like you are. The things which attack me to keep me from continuing on are the same things which come against you to keep you from continuing on. You and I have had many opportunities to throw in the towel and quit. We all overcome barriers the same way — through Jesus, the Word, and the power of the Holy Spirit.

> **Wherefore seeing we also are compassed about with so great a cloud of witnesses, let us lay aside every weight, and the sin which doeth so easily beset us, and let us run with patience the race that is set before us.**
>
> **Hebrews 12:1**

If something is attacking your life, and the devil is opposing the good in your life and trying to talk you into quitting, think about this great cloud of witnesses. Begin to associate yourself with winners who have continued in the face of opposition and have inherited and received the promise. That cloud of witnesses is made up of those testifying to the faithfulness of God. Begin to associate with people who are testifying to the faithfulness of God. Don't hang around with a bunch of people who say, "It won't work."

They are liars. They don't know what they're talking about. Lying vanities have overtaken them. Hang around with people who say, "It works." Plenty of people say the Word of God doesn't work. But they are the ones not receiving the promises. Hang around those who are receiving and inheriting the promises of God. You will find, time and time again, that there are ingredients in their lives which have caused them to possess the promises.

Once you get a good solid inspired thought from God, one good sound idea, and a good sound scripture, don't let go of it. When you know it's from God, and it just fits what you're believing God for, don't let go of it. Because that's the scripture which will put you over. That is the Word which will put you over.

Hebrews 12:1 says, **Let us lay aside every weight, and the sin which doth so easily beset us.** You could say, "Let's lay aside every encumbrance, or anything that would short out the circuit, so to speak." Lay aside anything that would hinder you from continuing on with God.

When you're believing God for certain things in your life, look around and see if the Spirit of God can show you anything that is hindering you. Look for anything which may be shorting out the circuit. Sin is missing the mark or anything that would keep you from continuing as a doer of the Word. Lay whatever it is aside. Get rid of it. Cast all your care upon Him. (1 Pet. 5:7.) Let Him take the load. Jesus told us this:

> Come unto me, all ye that labour and are heavy laden, and I will give you rest.
>
> Take my yoke upon you, and learn of me; for I am meek and lowly in heart: and ye shall find rest unto your souls.
>
> For my yoke is easy, and my burden is light.
>
> Matthew 11:28-30

Ye shall find rest unto your souls (v. 29). You shall have peace of mind when you begin to lay upon Jesus the weights and the things which would beset you. Then you will have the strength to carry on. Common hindrances are procrastination, lack of interest or lukewarmness, indecision, fear of criticism, and lack of organized plans.

When God gives you a direction, that's the time to move. When those 100-fold nuggets show up, that's the time to act upon them. Don't procrastinate. Be interested in the ideas God puts in your mind. If you have a hard time making a decision, get the facts and get rid of indecision. Fear of criticism is another opposition to being successful in ministry or business or even in your home.

Don't lack organized plans. Some think they can be scatterbrained and everything will fall out of the sky on their head. It doesn't happen that way. The devil will see to it that everything will work to stop your life. You must become determined and find the scriptures you're going to apply to your life. I've talked to ministers who are unorganized. They don't accomplish much.

I've thought about the ministers whom God is using mightily. Each one of them has good planning and good organization. They know where they'll be at this time next year. Some say, "That cuts out the Holy Spirit." Not necessarily. He still has plenty of opportunities to direct those advance plans, to minister through the smoothness of operation, and to still open doors unexpectedly.

What about Matthew 6:25 and 31 which say in essence, "Take no thought, for earthly needs, for God provides"? That really means to have no anxious concern or worry. Getting some plans will get rid of most anxious concern. Most people have a lot of anxious concern because they don't know what will happen next. But, if you have plans made, you've gotten rid of that anxious concern and have opened up channels for God to bless you and meet your needs.

Get rid of the things in your life which would hinder you. Here are 10 suggestions that will help you be able to train yourself to be persistent and patient, continuing to do the Word of God:

1. *Know exactly what you want.* Some people don't know what they want. Years later, they still don't know. Be specific with God. When you pray and talk to Him, talk to Him. Tell Him what's on your mind. If you don't remember what you talked to Him about, write it down so you won't forget. I know God is not going to forget, but write it down so *you* won't forget.

Know what you want and desire. Many ministers don't know where they are going. Years ago, there was a minister who didn't have anything going. He loved Jesus with all of his heart. He was telling people about Jesus all over town. But his ministry never really got off the ground. He was at a car lot one day. The car salesman was an old sinner to whom this man had presented the gospel.

The salesman said, "I don't believe what you're pitching. But you do. And you need to get yourself more organized and planned out. You need to get yourself set up right on this trying to lead people to Jesus. You need a couple of brochures. You need to get organized."

Know who that minister was? Bill Bright, founder and still head of Campus Crusade for Christ. That ministry now has thousands of missionaries all over the world because a sinner once told Bill Bright he needed to get his act together and get organized. You know, God can speak through donkeys. He can write on walls. He can speak through sinners.

Bill Bright got specific about what he wanted to do. He wanted to reach people on college campuses. And that's when he organized himself. He had a definite major purpose in that direction. He was not shooting in all directions. Things began to happen for him, but not until he got organized.

Another example is Jerry Falwell. He believes in reaching this nation through television. He believes in education. He has developed one of the largest television churches in America. In fact, his ministry is similar in several ways to Word of Faith World Outreach Center. He also has one of the largest churches in the United States and a Bible college and correspondence courses.

While we don't fully agree on all his doctrines, we do agree on reaching the world for Jesus. He gets people born again and helps them grow and mature as Christians. His ministry is organized, and he is a good steward of what God has placed in his hands. Jerry Falwell has been faithful. He began on television years ago. His TV ministry didn't amount to much, but the seed was sown, and he kept watering the seed. He was persistent and exercised himself in patience. Now his is one of the largest and most successful television audiences in the country. Why? Because he continued, he got specific, and he worked his plan. He had strong desire. He was organized. He got the besetting things and encumbrances out of the way, and now God has blessed him.

Kenneth Copeland has been faithful and diligent and organized with radio and rallies. He spent years with radio rallies. He was consistent and persistent. He exercised patience in what he was doing. He has given God plenty of opportunity to bless him.

T. L. Osborn has been faithful in missions — missions, missions, and more missions. He got specific. He designed out what he was going to do. He knew he was called. He knew he had the Word. And he knew God had called him to reach people. He got specific. He designed a plan.

> **A man's heart deviseth his way: but the Lord directeth his steps.**
>
> **Proverbs 16:9**

> **Roll your works upon the Lord — commit and trust them wholly to Him; [He will cause your thoughts to become agreeable to His will, and] so shall your plans be established and succeed.**
>
> **Proverbs 16:3 AMP**

God will give you inspired thoughts which are in agreement with His will. And if you act upon those inspired thoughts, they will always succeed. Notice that I used examples from different types of ministries. They are all successful because truth is where you find it. Be a good steward of all that God gives you. Stewardship applies to your house, your car, your clothes, as well as your ministry work. When you have a nice car, you should keep it clean. You should take care of it. If you take care of what you have, God will bless you with better things.

2. *Have a strong desire.* The scriptural references to desire point to a longing for, a wish, a want or a craving. You must have a strong longing or a strong want or a craving. It's like pecan pie. There are times when

I have a strong desire for pecan pie. I enjoy yogurt and chocolates and other sweets but, until I eat a good piece of pecan pie, that craving or longing is not satisfied.

> **Lord, all my desire is before thee; and my groaning is not hid from thee.**
>
> **Psalm 38:9**

> **Likewise, the Spirit also helpeth our infirmities: for we know not what we should pray for as we ought: but the spirit itself maketh intercession for us with** *groanings* **which cannot be uttered.**
>
> **Romans 8:26**

The Spirit of God *desires* so much to help us that He *groans* in such a way that it cannot be uttered. That is strong desire. That is a strong want. That is a strong craving. We need to have that same desire in our lives in order to achieve success.

3. *Have confidence in the Greater One within you.* Know that you know this:

> **I can do all things through Christ which strengtheneth me.**
>
> **Philippians 4:13**

> **I have strength for all things in Christ Who empowers me — I am ready for anything and equal to anything through Him Who infuses inner strength into me, [that is, I am self-sufficient in Christ's sufficiency.]**
>
> **Philippians 4:13** AMP

Philippians 4:13 is one of my favorite verses. "I can do all things through Christ." You don't get up some days to attack the kinds of giants I do and expect to win, to be able to cut off their heads, if you've been feeding only on "spiritual milk" and not confessing and standing upon God's Word. Only if the Word of God is in your mouth will you chop off those heads. So I start the day by saying this:

> Bless God, I can do all things today. I have the strength
> to do everything I need to do today. I can do all things
> today. I can do all things, because Christ is strengthen-
> ing me. Christ is giving me the strength to do whatever
> I must do to get the job done today and to continue
> on in the position in which God has placed me.

When you start talking like that, you start believing it, God starts believing it, the devil starts believing
it, the angels start believing it, and things happen,
praise God. And not until then do things happen.

4. *Any enterprise is built by wise planning.* Any enterprise becomes strong through common sense, and
profits by keeping abreast of the facts. (Prov. 24:3,4 TLB.)
An enterprise is a venture. Any venture, any project,
any enterprise is built by wise planning (v. 3).

Have a good set of organized plans. This may
sound secular. But it is also Bible truth: **For which of
you, intending to build a tower, sitteth not down first,
and counteth the cost, whether he have sufficient to
finish it?** (Luke 14:28). If you want to be a successful
person, you must feed on Word teachings. It isn't pie
in the sky. It is the application of God's Word. It is
wisdom with prudence.

5. *Have sufficient knowledge for what you're believing
God for.* This is another place where Christians miss it.
This is the area where training in patience and persistence pays off. If you want to start a certain business,
you need to find out about that particular business.
Take the time to find out the details. Do some research
before you jump into anything. Then, after you get sufficient knowledge, do the best you can, and God will
make up the difference. You will make mistakes. We
all do, but you can learn from those mistakes and not
repeat them. Analyze your mistake. What went wrong?

Why didn't your plan work? By using prudence and wisdom, you will find that whatever you put your hand to will always prosper.

I've been following the Lord for quite a few years now. And I've seen Christians do some of the most stupid things you can imagine. I've done some stupid things, and I don't like it. I don't like it at all. I like using prudence and wisdom, so that whatever I put my hand to always prospers.

You can learn from other people's successes. You can learn from the things they have done wrong. If you've had a failure or two, perhaps you can learn better from the things *you* did wrong. At the very least, you have learned not to do those things again. Analyze things. Why did they go wrong? Why didn't your plan work? Add this to your storehouse of knowledge.

6. *Work with other members of the Body of Christ.* Don't hesitate to draw strength and knowledge from what others know. The 12th chapter of Romans talks about the motive gift of leadership (or ruling), then it refers to the gifts of helps, mercy, giving, and others. What it boils down to is that we are many members and not all of us have the same position. **So we, being many, are one body in Christ, and every one members one of another** (Rom. 12:5).

So we must learn to work with other people. Don't be an island unto yourself. God may have given to others some knowledge that you don't have. He may have given it to them just so they can help you as you work together. For example, I don't know a great deal about electronics, but we have several experts on our staff and in our congregation. I don't say, "I'm going to do it." I let them do it, and it works. Work with other people who have some knowledge. But here is a warning: *Cheap knowledge is expensive.* Very expensive.

7. *Meditate on God's Word continually.* Meditate on your plan — on what you believe God has called you to do. Know it inside and out. Get it down into your spirit. When it goes from your head down into your heart, then it can really begin to work for you.

Daniel fasted and prayed for 21 days. Psychologists say it takes about 19 to 23 days of dealing with a new fact or new information before you become accustomed to it. If you move to a new house, it will take about 21 days before you become accustomed to that house. A new car would take about 21 days to become accustomed to. The same is true with things from God's Word.

What if you seek God for 21 days on specific items and areas of study? When the Word goes from your head down into your spirit, then you really have it. You must first get it into your mind. But when it gets down into your heart, then it really works for you. Fasting and prayer can reinforce the Word of God. It can reinforce in your spirit what God has called you to do.

8. *Overcome fear of criticism.* Don't worry about what other people might think or say. Your desire must be stronger than what other people think and say about you. Do you have that strong a desire to inherit the promises? To receive the reward? To receive the compensation? To receive what God has for you? To be successful? If the concern about what others think and say about you is stronger than your desire to receive the promises, then forget it, because you won't get anything.

James 1:8 says, **A double minded man is unstable in all his ways.** The desire in your heart must be so strong that you stay with it, no matter what anyone else may say. You might as well face this fact: Anytime you do anything different from the rest of the crowd, then you will catch some criticism. If you do anything, you'll be criticized. If you do nothing, you'll be criticized. When you endeavor to do anything for God or in business, there will be criticism and opportunities for the devil to try to talk you into quitting.

I don't believe, "If the door opens, it's God." I do believe this: If it is scriptural, it's God, whether or not the door is open. If you are a doer of the Word, that Word attracts criticism. But I want you to know it is the greatest thing in the world to be a doer of the Word and to be successful. And the Word of God will regulate your life for success.

> **Ask, and it shall be given you; seek, and ye shall find; knock, and it shall be opened unto you:**
>
> **For every one that asketh receiveth; and he that seeketh findeth; and to him that knocketh it shall be opened.**
>
> **Matthew 7:7,8**

In the Sermon on the Mount, Jesus said to rejoice when people persecute you because of the gospel. **Rejoice, and be exceeding glad: for great is your reward in heaven** (Matt. 5:12). In the next verse, Jesus says you are the salt of the earth. If you are salty, if you are the flavoring and the preservation of the earth, you're going to catch some criticism. If you're not salty, you're good for nothing but to be cast underfoot, He said.

God created man to be successful, but man failed. He missed the mark. Man was a failure. So God sent Jesus to recover us from failure and to restore us to that position of being successful in what He had created us to do. He wanted His plan to be successful. He didn't want His plan to fail. But God made man a free moral agent and gave him some guidelines. And man missed the mark. Before the foundation of the world, God knew man would miss it, and He came up with another plan. That plan was to send Jesus. Through Jesus, we were given the strength and power to be successful, regardless of the criticism we may receive.

Now let's look at the role of faith. God wants His plan to be successful. God wants the things He hoped for and the things He desired to come to pass. He desired for man to live in the Garden of Eden, to till the land, to enjoy achievement, and enjoy the things he hoped for. God also hoped for things. He had a plan. He had desires. He hoped they would come to pass, but they received a setback, a delay in the Garden of Eden.

So what did God do? He brought to man this spiritual ingredient known as faith. Faith gives substance to things hoped for. God gave us the measure of His faith so that His desires and dreams could come to pass in us. That is beautiful. God does take pleasure in your prosperity. God does take pleasure when His faith is working in your life. He does take pleasure when you succeed, because that is also His hopes, dreams, and desires coming to pass!

9. *Harness your mind.* Get victory over your thought life. Don't allow thoughts of failure to come into your mind. Don't allow thoughts of not making it, not having enough, of nobody liking you, of the negative things people are saying about you, to come into your mind. Philippians 4:8 says we are to think about things that are true, honest, just, pure, lovely, and of good

report: **If there be any virtue, and if there be any praise, think on these things.** Think on things that are good and clean and pure. Think on the positive things of God's Word.

Harness your thoughts. Your dominating thoughts control your life. What you think is what you become. **As he** (a man) **thinketh in his heart, so is he** (Prov. 23:7). Out of the abundance of whatever you have deposited in your heart, your mouth shall speak. (Matt. 12:34.) Whatever comes out of your mouth shall be produced in your life. (Mark 11:23.) That's strong. It's the Bible. Words are so important. We must learn to use this spiritual power given us by God. He doesn't want us to be children. He wants us to be mature adults. He wants us to enjoy seeing His Word fulfilled and working in our lives.

Later, we'll study creative visualization. We'll see that hope is a mental image. We'll see how to have creative, inspired thoughts, then see them come to pass. For that, you must be a free creature. Your spirit man must be free in order for you to have any liberty. Liberty looses the rivers of living waters to flow out of you. (John 7:38.)

You can't be bound or restrained and expect to be creative. These truths of who you are in Christ, and a good, clear, mental self-image or God-kind of image within you will begin to release God in you. If you're still bound by fear and worry and problems and lack and sickness, it's just as hard to get off the ground. But the Word of God will loose you from those things. Then you can be a free spirit and become inspired, and the Spirit of God can begin to flow through you.

Experts say the least creative time in your life is when you are bound. You are the most creative when you are the freest and the happiest and the most at peace. When you are walking in peace with no worries, and your point of view and perspective is correct, then the inspiration of the Almighty can come forth. You are not limited by the devil. You are not limited by saying, "I can't," because you're saying, "I can." And God begins to give you things you can do.

10. *Have someone stand in agreement with you.* This is extremely important. Have someone stand in agreement with you on what you're doing. **A threefold cord is not quickly broken** (Eccl. 4:12). When Jesus commissioned the disciples and sent them out, he sent them two by two. Have someone stand in agreement with you on what you're doing. There is little worse than going forth by yourself with nobody in agreement. As your enterprise grows larger, you'll have more people in agreement with you. In other words, you want to surround yourself with people who believe in what you're doing.

Don't let any negative doubter be around you. Don't hang around with them. You can love them and give them the Word, but don't hang around with losers and downers . . . negative people! Hang around with people who are working the Word. Do you know what will happen? Their success will rub off onto you. Pretty soon, your success will be rubbing off onto others. Success breeds success.

Find someone to stand in agreement with you. Find someone to agree with you in your business endeavors and whatever else you're involved in. My mom and dad were our agreement partners when Marte and I started in our ministry. Dad said, "Bob, I'll help you. I'll stand with you. I believe God has called you into the ministry."

Do you know who failed to stand with us? Many believers. They said, "You shouldn't go out there. You shouldn't do it." You know, I just started sticking my fingers into my ears, so to speak, on everything they said because I *knew* God had called me. When it was time to go into the ministry, God spoke to me. My wife agreed with me, and it's a good thing she did!

Marte and I have drawn tremendous strength from each other as we have stood in agreement with what God has called us to do. Of course, Jesus is in the middle or midst of such agreement. (Matt. 18:20.) That is a threefold cord of Marte and me with Jesus in the middle. And a threefold cord is not quickly broken. So have at least one other person stand with you. More is better. But if you have a big crowd in agreement, there is the possibility that some snakes will sneak in there. So it's better to keep it fairly small and strong rather than many and weak.

To use the Word of Faith World Outreach Center again as an example: We are in agreement to reach the city, the nation, and the world for Jesus. Our congregation knows there is a price to pay if we are to accomplish that goal. It takes more than being lukewarm, just showing up every now and then, and tithing when it's convenient. It takes the quality commitment from everyone in this church to be doers of the Word. We have that, and that's why it is working for us. That's why we're doing all that we're doing. We are all in agreement with the Word of God to do what God has called us to do.

> If two of you on earth agree (harmonize together, together make a symphony) about — anything and everything — whatever they shall ask, it will come to pass and be done for them by My Father in heaven.

> **For wherever two or three are gathered (drawn together as My followers) in (into) My name, there I AM in the midst of them.**
>
> **Matthew 18:19,20** AMP

With one or more in agreement, you are in harmony like an orchestra. That is when things begin to happen. That is when it is the most powerful. That's what happened on the day of Pentecost. Remember, **they were all with one accord** (Acts 2:1). They were in agreement. That's when the power came — when they were in agreement. The power comes when you find someone to agree with you. Jesus said that if two or more were gathered together in His name, He would be there. (Matt. 18:20.) When He is there, His power is there. And we don't want to be in agreement with anything except what Jesus is in agreement with.

> **You see that [his] faith was cooperating with his works, and [his] faith was completed and reached its supreme expression [when he implemented it] by [good] works.**
>
> **James 2:22 AMP**

Isn't that beautiful? His faith was completed and reached full maturity when he implemented it by his good works. Of course, he had to continue being a doer of the Word or he wouldn't have inherited the promise.

> **That ye be not slothful, but followers of them who through faith and patience inherit the promises.**
>
> **Hebrews 6:12**

Jesus said to continue in His Word. Continue being a doer. Do not become slothful, or lazy, or a quitter. Win through faith and patience, being steadfast and immovable, continually abounding in the work of the Lord. Those are the ones who inherit the promises. Do you want to inherit the promises? This is how.

And not everything that sparkles is gold. But there is an elite, elect group of real born-again, blood-washed believers, and they are the ones inheriting the promises. Then there are the tares. Tares are weeds which look like wheat. They are deceiving plants. They are found out by their lack of fruit at harvest time. The Bible is very clear about tares. It's very clear about wolves in sheep's clothing. It's very clear and specific about those things. Make sure there isn't some false angel of light in your life trying to steer you off course.

When Marte and I were first born again, there actually was a man who could tell us things that would happen the next few days. He would tell things that had happened weeks or years earlier in our lives. He preached Jesus to one group and reincarnation to another group.

I read in my Bible that **it is appointed unto man once to die, but after this the judgment** (Heb. 9:27). Aren't you glad that we don't come back again and again and again? Aren't you glad Jesus went one time to Calvary? Now through Him we are good enough to go all the way, praise God!

We were baby Christians, but we were the smart ones. Others were deceived, but not Marte and me. We put a stop to that entire teaching in our area. We started telling everyone what this person was saying and his whole group shipwrecked. He was a false prophet disguised as an angel of light. The woman who led us to the Lord saw him transparent and clear like an angel. The Lord spoke to her and told her he was an angel of light, a fallen angel. That's a demon. That's a high-ranking demon. And he looked like a man. He said a lot of good things, but his tongue was twisted and warped. It didn't line up with the Word of God.

We were new Christians at the time and knew
hardly anything about the Word. God was gracious
enough to let us find out how to get away from him.
Many people fell because of him. Some are still fallen.
Some to this day think he was right. But aren't you glad
God has given us the Word? We can walk in it. We can
walk in the light of God's Word.

> **But let patience have her perfect work, that ye may be
> perfect and entire, wanting nothing.**
>
> **James 1:4**

> **But let endurance and steadfastness and patience have
> full play and do a thorough work, so that you may be
> [people] perfectly and fully developed (with no
> defects), lacking in nothing.**
>
> **James 1:4 AMP**

If you let patience do her job, with your corresponding actions of faith you will inherit the promises
and you shall have what you are believing God for. That
is a good reason for letting patience have her perfect
work. It lets you get what you've been believing God
for. God's Word and God's grace are sufficient.

In your patience possess ye your souls (Luke 21:19)
— your mind, will, and emotions. When you start being
double-minded, your soul becomes unstable. It starts
vacillating back and forth. **A double minded man is
unstable in all his ways** (James 1:8). You must find a
promise, know what you're believing God for, put forth
corresponding actions of faith, and continue them until
you receive that promise. You'll then be entire and complete, wanting nothing.

This stabilizes your soul — your mind, will, and
emotions. When you start giving up, your mind starts
going haywire. People come to us for counseling whose
minds are haywire. They tell us they are believing the

Word, but we tell them they have stopped being a doer of the Word. They didn't let patience have her perfect work. For, if they had, their souls would have been normal.

Patience is similar to hope, and hope is the anchor of the soul, both sure and steadfast.

> **[Now] we have this [hope] as a sure and steadfast anchor of the soul — it cannot slip and it cannot break down under whoever steps out upon it — [a hope] that reaches farther and enters into [the very certainty of the Presence] within the veil,**
>
> **Where Jesus has entered in for us [in advance], a Forerunner having become a High Priest forever after the order [with the rank] of Melchizedek.**
>
> **Hebrews 6:19,20 AMP**

If your hope loses its picture and you stop seeing yourself as God sees you, you have nothing for faith to give substance to. Your soul (mind, will, emotions) will start flickering and jumping all around, because there is no anchor to hold it steady and give it stability. Even our video equipment is this way. We must have a signal going into that equipment or it gets the jitters. And people must have a signal of something for which they are believing God. **Where there is no vision, the people perish** (Prov. 29:18).

You must have something in which you are operating to channel that faith power through. If you have nothing to channel faith through, your whole life is full of jittery thoughts and emotions and ups and downs.

> **Casting down imaginations, and every high thing that exalteth itself against the knowledge of God, and bringing into captivity every thought to the obedience of Christ.**
>
> **2 Corinthians 10:5**

When you do that, you will always succeed. When you do that, you'll always win. And you will avoid the most common failure in the Body of Christ — lack of patience. In your persistence, you become a winner. Ephesians 6:13,14 says, **and having done all, to stand. Stand therefore.** Be immovable, always abounding in the Work of the Lord. (1 Cor. 15:58.)

6

THE LAW OF COMPENSATION

The Bible — the Book of all books — is God's text-book for success. If you will spend time searching the scriptures, you'll find that abundant life which Jesus has provided for us.

Heavenly Father, I thank You for the anointing which abides within me. It is the anointing of truth to break every yoke of darkness and unbelief and misunderstanding. I thank You, Father God, that these believers will read and they will receive the inspired Word. They will become more enlightened. They will graduate from glory to glory, from faith to faith. Father, I thank You for the success and the prosperity being received by each believer studying this. Thank You for Your Word. Thank You, Father, for the great things which lie in store for us. Thank You for the great opportunities that You are now preparing us to be able to receive. In Jesus' name. Amen.

That last portion of the prayer above was extremely prophetic. It illuminated in my spirit. God said, "I am preparing you for the great opportunities that lie ahead." If we'll take advantage of this preparation, we will be ready to receive the things God is going to send our way — whether it be opportunities to minister salvation or the infilling of the Holy Spirit or bringing healing to other people or being personally led into profitable business ventures.

God is preparing our spirit man to be able to receive opportunities that lie ahead. If you are a 30-fold, a 60-fold, or a 100-fold Christian, you know the necessity of proper planning, information, and meditation. That is the process God has directed us to show you. As we've already learned, *success* means "to obtain a desired end" or "to have a favorable outcome." We all want those, don't we? To *succeed* means "to achieve the results hoped for and to receive the things planned."

We might add one more thought to that: Success is the power or ability to obtain favorable results. Good information gives you the power or the ability to obtain successful results. In fact, you must have the power to obtain favorable results. That power comes by hearing and hearing by or through the Word of God.

You are a spirit creature. You are a God-kind of creature. You've been created in the image of God. God is spirit, soul, and body. You are spirit, soul and body. We've not received our glorified bodies, but we're well on our way!

> Though our outward man perish, yet the inward man is renewed day by day.
>
> **2 Corinthians 4:16**

Compensation means "an equal return for something given." The archaic word for compensation is *recompense*. Both words mean the same thing, "a giving back to." God's law of compensation is the law of "giving back to." You might call it wages. When you work, you're compensated for your efforts. You're given wages or payment. You earn it. Wages are a medium of exchange for labor. You exchange your time, talent, and energy (physical and mental) for a specified amount of money. You're compensated or recompensed for your efforts.

Let's turn to the Book of beginnings, Genesis, and let's look at the law of compensation revealed by God in the very first chapter:

> And God said, Let the earth bring forth grass, the herb yielding seed, and the fruit tree yielding fruit after

his kind, whose seed is in itself, upon the earth: and it was so.

And the earth brought forth grass, and herb yielding seed after his kind, and the tree yielding fruit, whose seed was in itself, after his kind: and God saw that it was good.

Genesis 1:11,12

It was good, not evil. It was designed to be good. When God said, **Let the earth bring forth,** (v. 11) He meant it! This earth has been commissioned by God to yield or to bring forth. Truth is truth, wherever you find it and whoever is using it. Many people in the world have used this truth or principle. They go out and begin to sow some effort into a particular business which then yields and brings forth and gives back a return on their efforts.

This earth is commissioned by God to bring forth. So the herb yields a seed. It gives back. The fruit tree yields fruit. Through that yield, it gives back after its kind. The herb yields seed and the fruit tree yields fruit, each after its kind. Everything reproduces after its kind. Each operates in the law of compensation.

This law is even true in Word of Faith World Outreach Center. It is reproducing after its kind. We're reproducing the Word of God, *the word of faith*, righteousness, our identification or oneness with Christ, prosperity, healing, divine health. We are reaching the city, the nation, and the world with God's truth. We are establishing video Bible colleges. We are conducting television, radio, and satellite seminars. This particular church is reproducing after its kind.

God commissioned the earth to bring forth. He set in motion the herb to yield. That word *yield* means "to bring forth." The herb is to yield the seed and that seed gives back what was yielded. So the phrase, **yielding seed,** means that the seed *gives back*. Compensation means "that which is given back." Then God brought forth man, and man was also to give back:

> And God said, Let us make man in our image, after
> our likeness: and let them have dominion over the fish
> of the sea, and over the fowl of the air, and over the
> cattle, and over all the earth, and over every creeping
> thing that creepeth upon the earth.
>
> > Genesis 1:26

God yielded or brought forth man in His image, after His kind. Man originally was a God-kind of creature. Adam was as a god here in this earth. Man, of course, forfeited or yielded that dominion, that God-kind of authority, to Satan. Then Satan became the *god* of this world. (2 Cor. 4:4.) Through disobedience, man yielded or lost his dominion.

> So God created man in his own image, in the image
> of God created him; male and female created he them.
>
> And God blessed them, and God said unto them . . . .
>
> > Genesis 1:27,28

Satan is a fallen angel and still has some supernatural power, but not God's kind of power. Then, of course, Adam forfeited his dominion over the earth, his God-delegated authority, to Satan who became a *god* of this world. I repeat, this did not make Satan *God* or all-powerful, all-knowing, nor omnipresent, any more than Adam had been. It did give him the title and authority of *god of this world*. Through disobedience, man lost his authority to be in charge of the earth. He lost dominion.

God spoke to the earth, "Earth, you bring forth." Next, God spoke to the grass and to the herbs. "Grass, herbs, you bring forth seed." Then God said, "Fruit trees, you give back. Earth, you give back." God blessed man and said, "Multiply and replenish. Man, you give back."

> And God blessed them, and God said unto them, Be fruitful, and multiply, and replenish the earth, and subdue it: and have dominion over the fish of the sea, and over the fowl of the air, and over every living thing that moveth upon the earth.
>
> **Genesis 1:28**

So there's a law involved here, the law of compensation. Not only does it work in the plant world in the earth, but it also works through man. This is the basic law of "giving back." This is a simple message. I want you to totally understand this law. Then you need to put it to work in your life and use it. It's there, designed by God for your use. In fact, it *has* been working in your life, whether or not you realize it. Everything reproduces after its own kind. There is always a giving back or a replenishing of its own kind. Everybody wants to reap more good and less evil. I know you're all for that. A perfect example of this is found in Genesis 8:

> While the earth remaineth, seedtime and harvest, and cold and heat, and summer and winter, and day and night shall not cease.
>
> **Genesis 8:22**

Let me ask you a question: Is the earth still here? Yes, of course it is. Well, then this law must still be in operation. It says "as long as the earth remains," there will be a seedtime and a time to harvest, a time to sow and a time to reap. In other words, there will be a giving back, a compensation. As long as the earth remains, there will be a giving back, a compensation for what is sown, a giving back or a recompense.

> To every thing there is a season, and a time to every purpose under heaven:

**A time to be born, and a time to die; a time to plant,
and a time to pluck up that which is planted.**

Ecclesiastes 3:1,2

There is a time to plant (to give) and there is a time to pluck up (to receive back what was given). The farmer sows a seed. Then harvest time comes, the time for giving back. The earth has been commissioned to give back what was sown. This is the law of all laws, including the royal law of love. If you sow love, you will get love given back to you. So the law of all laws is the law of compensation, the law of return, the law of action and reaction.

God set it in motion in Genesis, the Book of beginnings. It is here. And you've been reaping the results of that law. If you haven't been reaping the type of results you want to reap, then begin now to change that by lining up more with the good side, instead of the evil side.

**Be not deceived; God is not mocked: for whatsoever
a man soweth, that shall he also reap.**

Galatians 6:7

Be not deceived or beguiled. Eve was beguiled in the Garden of Eden. Eve said, "The serpent beguiled me. He told me I would become as God, knowing good and evil. He deceived me." The word *deceive* comes from the same root word as *deceit*. When people are deceitful, they try to beguile someone. *Deceit* or *guile* refers to the planting of some type of false idea.

God tells us not to allow Satan to inject any false ideas into our lives and thinking. God is not mocked. He is not laughed at. God has not forgotten His Word. He has not forgotten His promises. God said, **Whatsoever a man soweth, that shall he also reap** (Gal. 6:7).

If God said something, it is still coming to pass today. The law of compensation, for good or for bad, is always there. Whatever a man sows or gives, that shall he also reap or be compensated with.

Let me define the word *sow*. *To sow* means "to plant seed for growth." When seed is planted for growth, there will be a coming up and then a return from that seed. To sow can also mean "to scatter." To sow is to set in motion.

> Happy and fortunate are you who cast your seed upon all waters [when the river overflows its banks; for the seed will sink into the mud and when the waters subside will spring up; you will find it after many days in an abundant harvest], and can safely send forth the ox and the donkey [to range freely].
>
> Isaiah 32:20 AMP

> Cast thy bread upon the waters: for thou shalt find it after many days.
>
> Ecclesiastes 11:1

This command to cast your bread upon the waters and it will come back after many days means that there is a giving (sowing) and there is a getting back (reaping) equivalent to what was given. There is a compensation. That verse does not say you will receive *more* in return, but an amount equivalent to what you sowed. When you sow little, you get little. When you sow much, you get much.

> Give, and it shall be given unto you; good measure, pressed down, and shaken together, and running over, shall men give into your bosom. For with the same measure that ye mete withal it shall be measured to you again.
>
> Luke 6:38

So when you give, you're setting some things into motion. What you set into motion depends on what you gave. You have the power to sow, to scatter, to set things into motion. What have you been putting into motion? Have you been wanting to put more things into motion or less? If you had your choice, would you stop or slow down a few things which are in motion? And would you speed up some others?

To sow can also mean "to introduce into an environment." *When you sow the Word by speaking the Word, you are introducing something spiritual into the physical realm.* You're putting a spiritual force into motion to bring about something physical. To sow is to introduce into an environment, to implant, or to set in motion.

> For with what judgment ye judge, ye shall be judged: and with what measure ye mete, it shall be measured to you again.
>
> Ask, and it shall be given you; seek, and ye shall find; knock, and it shall be opened unto you:
>
> For every one that asketh receiveth; and he that seeketh findeth; and to him that knocketh it shall be opened.
>
> Matthew 7:2,7,8

When you use wise planning and ask, you set things into motion, and you shall receive. When you seek, you shall find. When you knock — again, setting things into motion — it shall be opened unto you. There is a compensation. Whatever a person sets in motion, whatever he implants into his environment, that shall he also reap or receive back. If you want to walk in the dominion given us as God-kind of creatures, then you must believe along these lines.

Our Blessings Are Just Beginning

I believe we have scarcely begun to tap into the potential power we have as spirit beings, as God-kind of beings. We've scarcely begun to receive those bless-ings so numerous **that there shall not be room enough to receive** (them) (Mal. 3:10). Praise God, these truths cause my sights to become higher every day. What the spirit of man can believe, he can always receive.

How many times have you drawn a picture you really like? After you were finished with it, did you look at it a few times? Perhaps you put it where you could look at it some more as you worked. There was something compelling about it. You were seeing something that had been on the inside of you. It had appealed to your spirit man who had prompted you to create it. It's so exciting to realize that God gave the spirit of man the capability of reproducing, as well as the body. The spirit of man has the ability to sow and to receive back what is sown. This is exciting and fulfill-ing and rewarding.

If you haven't done so today, take time to be creative. That is success, to create out of your spirit.

We've defined the word *sow*, now let's take the word *reap*. *To reap* means "to gather together, to obtain something that was set in motion (sowed)." *To reap* is to obtain the end results of what you sowed. And that is exciting, as long as it is positive. *To reap* also means "to win" or "to possess." The older, archaic English meaning of to reap was "to succeed' or "to receive desires hoped for." So reaping is God's law of compen-sation.

The law is impartial, however, so that whatever is sown is what will be reaped. If you sow doubt, unbelief, hate, or other negative things, you'll reap those things. They bring failure, but you're still suc-ceeding in reaping what you've sown.

Cast not away therefore your confidence, which hath great recompence of reward.

For ye have need of patience, that, after ye have done the will of God, ye might receive the promise.

Hebrews 10:35,36

Notice that your confidence has a great recompence of reward. There is the giving back. After you have released the Word in your environment, then compensation comes. There is the receiving back of what you've sown. These are important days to be operating in this law. Now is the time to make it operate in our favor.

Some say, "What are we going to do? We don't have enough. Interest rates are going up. We can't afford to buy a car. There isn't enough gasoline, and it's too expensive."

If God's law is true, what will you be receiving if you talk like that? Lack. If there ever was a time to speak plenty, and to speak success, and to speak what God's Word says about blessings and divine health and having more than enough to meet every need, that time is now! Now is the time to talk abundance and act on your words. But if you begin to see lack and talk lack, then lack is what you'll reap.

Let me give you an example of what happens when you talk lack. I know some people who've lived in a little rundown shack for about 25 years. Progress has grown up around them. They said, "We can't afford another house. They are just so expensive. We had better stay right here."

What happened? They shorted out their receiving. That kind of thinking caused them to become dormant and that is where they are going to stay. The earth will not yield anything else for them as long as they remain in that position.

My spirit man is growing. I am capable of believing God for more things today than yesterday. Furthermore, I am going to be capable of receiving more desired results from God tomorrow than I am today, because Jesus is Lord. Jesus is my Lord. He is my Shepherd, and I don't want. I don't have lack. No matter what happens to interest rates, or the price of automobiles, gasoline, food, furniture, or clothes, I will always have my share and have more than enough, because I have chosen to look into the perfect law of liberty!

Since God's law of compensation works and everything reproduces after its own kind, when you say, "There is not enough," then the first thing you will receive is portions of "not enough" or lack and want.

People said to me, "What are you doing out there in north Dallas where the property value is skyrocketing all around? How in the world can you build those church buildings and buy all that property?"

And the devil tells me this, "You should be off somewhere back of the tracks in a metal building with a gravel parking lot. You'll never make it in north Dallas. God is not big enough to do that."

My God is! He told me, "Go to Farmers Branch." He knew where He was sending us. Everything we need has been supplied. It doesn't matter whether it is skyscrapers or tin barns, God has the power to make it work out. I heard a news report at the time we were constructing our auditorium in the late 1970s. A financial planner from Canada was being interviewed. Many

Canadians have invested in land in the Dallas area. He said Dallas is the capstone of the last frontier for commercial development. He said the area surrounding the freeway where we had bought land earlier and were building was the hottest real estate territory in the world at the time of that interview.

We're glad the Holy Spirit has set us right in the middle of that. And He has supplied every need. Jesus said not to let your candle be hidden, to set it where it would be plainly visible. (Matt. 5:15.) Knock that bushel basket off the top of your candle. Set your light where the greatest number of people can see it. More than 100,000 cars per day pass in front of our church and even more pass a few blocks south on an even busier freeway where we have billboards.

We've just begun to see what God will do through people who believe Him. It excites me. It inspires me. When man was totally obedient to God's laws, man reaped the compensation or rewards of that obedience. They were the blessings of life — eternal life, walking with God, health, happiness, success, and prosperity. Obedience releases the reward of blessings. When you obey the law, you reap the rewards.

But when man was disobedient, he broke his tie with God. The penalty of disobedience is the curse, which was death, sickness, sorrow, failure, and poverty. **For the wages of sin is death** (Rom. 6:23). Disobedience releases the curse — calamities, problems, trials, and distresses. When you disobey the law, you reap the penalties.

The world strives to get something for nothing. But *there is no such thing as something for nothing*. Everyone wants something for nothing, but everything has a cost.

It is unscriptural to get something for nothing. The law of compensation as revealed in the Bible is that something reproduces something and nothing reproduces nothing. The two cannot switch because something will never reproduce nothing, and nothing will never reproduce something. There's no such thing as something for nothing. But there is something for something. As you go forth, applying effort to advance the Kingdom of God, you shall obtain a return.

Many Christians think that faith is doing nothing. They think that faith is just sitting around waiting for the pie in the sky to land on their heads, or that life is going to be better on the other side of the fence. When that doesn't work, they start praying that Jesus will come that very day and rescue them. That's just laziness. I know Jesus is coming, but we are supposed to be doing a few things before He comes. That does not include "just waiting on the Lord" nor "just a-hoping and a-praying." We are to be up and about, doing something about what we prayed for and believed that we received. We are to take corresponding actions.

Ever since I was born again, I've known ministers, hundreds and hundreds of ministers. Early in this time, do you know where many of those ministers stayed? In coffee shops. They talked about the great revival that is going to come. I heard them prophesy it, "Well, one of these days, it's going to come." We believed that it was already here, so we went out and did something about bringing it here. We took corresponding action. Yet those same ministers are still doing nothing. They sowed nothing, and they reaped nothing.

That is true of some families I've known. And if you do nothing, you reap nothing. Be diligent and you will get plenty. Put your hand to the plow and don't look back. Keep on keeping on. Put out the Word of God. Keep sowing those seeds. According to God's Word, it has to come back!

> **He becometh poor that dealeth with a slack hand: but the hand of the diligent maketh rich.**
>
> **Proverbs 10:4**

Let me share something else with you. There is a way to increase your return on what you sow. When you're hired to do a job, you are compensated for what you were hired to do. Before you can be promoted at work, you must do at least what you were hired to do. But if you do more, then you'll be in line to receive more.

There Is a Way to Increase the Return

In other words, there is a way to increase the force of the law of compensation: It's called "going the extra mile." Look at Matthew 5 for a scriptural admonition to go the extra mile:

> **And whosoever shall compel thee to go a mile, go with him twain.**
>
> **Give to him that asketh thee, and from him that would borrow of thee turn not thou away.**
>
> **Matthew 5:41,42**

Whenever anyone hires you to do a job, go the "extra mile." Do more than you're paid to do, and you'll end up getting paid more. Be worth more than you're paid. That employer may not recognize it, but God will send along an employer who will pay you what you're worth. God's law of compensation must work. When you're hired to do a job and you do that job, then you're going to be compensated for exactly the hours that you worked. But if you go the extra mile and do more than you're being paid for, then you will increase your return of compensation.

Whatsoever a man soweth, that shall he also reap.
Galatians 6:7

He which soweth sparingly shall reap also sparingly; and he which soweth bountifully shall reap also bountifully.
2 Corinthians 9:6

By giving more, you open yourself to receive more back. Do you get as excited as I do about prospering? When I talk about prospering, I'm not talking about heaping up riches. I'm talking about seeing the promises come to fruition and enjoying seeing the Word attain results. Can you imagine going to church for 20 or 30 years and never seeing the Word of God work and bring results? How sad. No wonder people are leaving many of our churches. Even the leaders are admitting that mere religion is boring. I had that figured out by about age 16. I didn't know Christianity could be fulfilling through seeing the Word work. I thought what I saw was all there was to it!

God didn't give us all these promises just to have them lie around dormant. He wants these things to come alive in our lives. Seeing the Word work makes life worth living. *I don't have all the answers, but I've found the place where all the answers can be found.* Doing the Word opens your eyes even more. And the more you do, the more you understand. Those who never do anything, understand nothing. They never get that law of compensation working in their lives.

Get that compensation principle working in your life. Start right where you are. Take what you know, begin working on it, and God will give you some more. He will give back to you. Just take one little truth and work it. You will be amazed at the results. It will be like a little seed and will begin growing.

Did you ever notice a little bud on a rose bush? You can see the bud, and you know there's a bloom inside. You can't see it, so you don't know what color the rose is. I felt in my spirit recently a "new bud" or a "limb" about to spring out. I just sensed it. I knew it was there, but I didn't know what it was. God was endeavoring to give birth to a new, inspired thought in my spirit. I started getting excited about giving birth.

We can be pregnant with something in our spirits. We are pregnant with the Word, expecting the physical manifestation. It's like a new baby. You don't know if it is a girl or a boy, until it's born. You know it's there, but you don't know what it is. The big day comes, and you say, "It's a girl!" Or you say, "It's a boy!"

Finally, the Holy Spirit began to bring this forth from my spirit. I saw it! I began to write it down. I captured what God was giving me. And God had given birth to a new branch, a new bud on the "tree" of my spirit. It was a new branch, like a new blossom, for our ministry. God's Word within is like that rose bud. It is a small beginning, but the end result will be an entire rose bush filled with beautiful flowers.

Start Where You Are

You must always start where you are. Start believing at your level of faith, not mine. Let the Word begin working more and stronger in your life. It does things for you beyond anything you thought would happen to you. Then your whole level of life changes. So plant those tiny seeds in your spirit. Act on what you know.

Also, some special things need to be done to care for new branches and blossoms. We need to exercise patience, do wise planning, continue to energize our spirits for creative thoughts, continue applying the Word of faith in our lives, and continue to let only God's Word be in our mouths. All of this brings forth that successful ministry branch or blossom. As this happens, you begin to discover the color of the rose in the blossom. You see a new ministry work in its fullness as it develops.

Length of days is in her (Wisdom's) **right hand; and in her left hand riches and honour.**

Proverbs 3:16

When you are faithful in small things, God will bless you later with much. Start at your level of faith and be faithful with that. For example, we once had the cheapest make of car one can buy. We began there. I still like that kind of car. At that time, that was our level of faith for transportation. Now it is higher, and we have that higher level of transportation. I'm not caught up in fancy cars. Yet through a chain of events, one right after the next, several years ago we started driving a new car every year. And it's cheaper than what we were paying for a lesser quality car. It just started happening. I was preaching the Word and acting on the Word. Things just started happening.

And I kept on preaching the Word and speaking the Word and acting on the Word. I kept patient. I kept doing Joshua 1:8. Then I began noticing good things showing up around me. I gave away a pair of shoes, then I noticed three or four pairs came back. I kept giving watches away, then I noticed a very expensive watch had "jumped onto" my wrist! I've been preaching and teaching the Word and principles of success. And from the windows of heaven, God just keeps dumping success on top of me. Have you had that happen to you?

Also, I praise God for a congregation that's not jealous of how God blesses its pastor. In fact, it's just the opposite. They want their pastor blessed. People who are jealous of those who are blessed of God are speaking and thinking things which block God's efforts to bless them. They confess and speak, "I can't." They give nothing and believe nothing and reap nothing.

Watch and imitate those for whom the Word is working. Watch and imitate those who succeed. Expect your pastor to succeed. Help him succeed. Let those principles start working in your life. We have people in our congregation who are successful now. Here is how they got to success and prosperity. They were consistently faithful at church. They attended, learned, and worked. They gave generously of what they had. Today these people have Christian maturity, successful jobs and businesses, new homes, and new cars, all because they were faithful with whatever they had. Now they have much.

I think of individuals who had a seed, just a small idea. They were faithful. They had a good product. They gave more than enough in service and effort. And they gave to the Lord. In very few years, such people have become more successful than they ever dreamed of becoming.

Take care of what you have now. Stay faithful. Keep on keeping on. Don't shut down for any person, any situation, or any circumstance. Just keep on keeping on with God's Word — God's textbook for success — and you will know success. You'll be living in divine health. You'll have the blessing of God. (Deut. 28.) You will be lending and not borrowing. We do borrow money. We have borrowed a lot. But the value of what we have is many times the value of what we owe. When we started, we had no money. We paid rent to people. Now we loan or give money to others, and people pay rent to us.

This achievement is a process. It just starts evolving and, before you know it, you are the head and not the tail, lending and not borrowing. Like dieting, this success doesn't happen overnight. People take years to get overweight, and they want to become skinny overnight. Likewise, people want to get rich overnight. Luke 6 illustrates the law of compensation perfectly:

> But I say unto you which hear, Love your enemies, do good to them which hate you.
>
> Bless them that curse you, and pray for them which despitefully use you.
>
> Luke 6:27,28

Why should we love and do good to our enemies, to those who hate us? Because of the law of compensation. When you do good to those who hate you, they'll end up loving you. What will happen if you pray for those who curse you? They will start blessing you. And even if they don't, God will. *The Amplified Bible* translates verse 28: **implore God's blessing (favor) upon those who abuse you — who revile, reproach, disparage, and high-handedly misuse you.** The law of compensation says you will then receive God's favor and blessing in return. They will stop using you and start taking care of you, or God will give you the reward of obedience.

> And unto him that smiteth thee on the one cheek offer also the other; and him that taketh away thy cloke forbid not to take thy coat also.

> Give to every man that asketh of thee; and of him that taketh away thy goods ask them not again.
>
> And as ye would that men should do to you, do ye also to them likewise.
>
> Luke 6:29-31

Why? Because of the law of compensation. It is God's law. It is sowing and reaping. Look at sowing and reaping. What you sow, you shall reap.

> Do not be deceived and deluded and misled; God will not allow Himself to be sneered at — scorned, disdained or mocked [by mere pretensions or professions, or His precepts being set aside]. — He inevitably deludes himself who attempts to delude God. For whatever a man sows, that and that only is what he will reap.
>
> For he who sows to his own flesh (lower nature, sensuality) will from the flesh reap decay and ruin and destruction; but he who sows to the Spirit will from the Spirit reap life eternal.
>
> And let us not lose heart and grow weary and faint in acting nobly and doing right, for in due time and at the appointed season we shall reap, if we do not loosen and relax our courage and faint.
>
> So then, as occasion and opportunity open to us, let us do good (morally) to all people [not only being useful or profitable to them, but also doing what is for their spiritual good and advantage]. Be mindful to be a blessing.
>
> Galatians 6:7-10 AMP

What you sow, you shall reap. That's why it is more blessed to give than to receive. The most profitable part of sowing is giving. The compensation comes from giving. There's no productivity in receiving. Productivity comes when you give because of the law of compensation.

Receiving Is Not the Most Profitable Part

Joy comes from giving — a joy like no other. Just be a blessing to everyone. Confess the Word and say, "I'm a blessing wherever I go." Because you are a blessing, you'll end up getting blessed more than the people you bless. Why? Because it comes back. I am usually one of the first to give. The more I give, the more I am loosing to return to me. I talk success, and I get success. I talk abundance, and I get abundance. I talk having buildings all over this city, and we end up having buildings all over this city.

Recently, I was thinking about someone we know who is barely getting by and, sometimes, has a really bad and sour attitude. This person wants to be better, but never puts the Word in his mouth. He never releases what he believes. He never sows anything to get back returns. When I say I'm a blessing everywhere I go, I'm not being egotistical. I'm simply confessing what I believe that I am. I want to be a blessing to you; therefore, I am a blessing everywhere I go. And I end up getting blessed more than the people I bless. Why? Because it comes back. I don't try to be a blessing just to get back. But it just comes back, because that is God's law. We really have something to give the world. Let's give it.

> But love your enemies, and be kind and do good — doing favors so that someone derives benefit from them; and lend expecting and hoping for nothing in return, but considering nothing as lost and despairing of no one; and then your recompense (your reward) will be great — rich, strong, intense and abundant — and you will be sons of the Most High; for He is kind and charitable and good to the ungrateful and the selfish and wicked.
>
> So be merciful — sympathetic, tender, responsive and compassionate — even as your Father is [all these].

> Judge not — neither pronouncing judgment nor sub-
> jecting to censure — and you will not be judged; do
> not condemn and pronounce guilty, and you will not
> be condemned and pronounced guilty; acquit and
> forgive and release (give up resentment, let it drop),
> and you will be acquitted and forgiven and released.
>
> Luke 6:35-37 AMP

Forgiveness fits into the law of compensation.
When you want God to forgive you, He said that first
you have to forgive. You release a person from
indebtedness to you, then God will release you of your
indebtedness.

> Give, and [gifts] will be given you, good measure,
> pressed down, shaken together and running over will
> they pour into [the pouch formed by] the bosom [of
> your robe and used as a bag]. For with the measure
> you deal out — that is, with the measure you use when
> you confer benefits on others — it will be measured
> back to you.
>
> Luke 6:38 AMP

Again we see the law of compensation. God set
the law of compensation in motion. It is here in the
earth. With the same measure that you give, it will be
measured back to you. Go the extra mile, and the extra
mile will be given to you. We want to bring ourselves
into remembrance of this.

> There are those who [generously] scatter abroad, and
> yet increase more; there are those who withhold more
> than is fitting or what is justly due, but it tends only
> to want.
>
> Proverbs 11:24 AMP

The law of compensation is illustrated in those who
scatter, yet increase more. *To withhold* means "to be
stingy or tight." *Withholding* means "having closed fists
or keeping your pocketbook closed." If you do that, it

will bring poverty and lack. The next verse says, **The liberal person shall be enriched, and he who waters shall himself be watered.** The word *liberal* also means "to grow." The growing soul shall be enriched. The giver is the one who is growing.

> The fruit of the [uncompromisingly] righteous is a tree of life, and he who is wise captures human lives for God [as a fisher of men] — he gathers and receives them for eternity.
>
> Behold, the [uncompromisingly] righteous shall be recompensed on the earth.
>
> **Proverbs 11:30,31** AMP

Where are the uncompromisingly righteous to be recompensed? *On earth.* That verse didn't say the righteous shall only be recompensed in heaven. It said the recompense would come **on the earth.** You must put away the religious attitude that it is a sin to prosper. The compensation is there. If God delights in my prosperity, then I want to prosper so God will delight in me. Thinking it is a sin to prosper is inaccurate thinking, programmed by the devil. Prosperity is an important portion of the covenant provided for us by God through Jesus Christ. It comes with the package.

If we're going to preach this gospel to the whole world, then a large number of believers must start getting their thinking right on prosperity. Then we pastors can have the funds to do what God has called us to do in reaching the whole world. We'll have the funds to do what God has called us to do only when we preach God's Word the way He told us to preach it. And that's along the lines of success and prosperity.

After sowing the Word into the people, the Word will begin to reproduce that success and prosperity in people's lives. They will know and experience that abundant life of which Jesus spoke: a life of success, prosperity, health, and total well-being. And the finances will be there.

The pastors who dare to preach God's Word, no matter what people say, are the ones expanding the outreach of their ministries. And believers who dare to believe God's Word and speak it and act upon it are the ones who are succeeding and prospering. It is the pastors' responsibility to teach this. Then, as we teach it, it will begin to grow in the congregations, and we'll have what we need to propagate the gospel.

You are destined to continual success in everything you do. There may be a few misconceptions. There may be some things not stressed just right. But it will all balance out and we shall continue. The Word will wash out the things that are not quite right and will keep on cleaning and producing and cleaning and producing. You have to start someplace. Start where you are and trust God to straighten things out. If you have carnal thinking about money, quit it. Start being spiritual. You don't want your possessions to possess you. You want to possess your possessions.

Ye cannot serve God and mammon (Luke 16:13). You cannot trust in riches, uncertain riches. But you can trust in the certain riches of God, then you'll also have the other riches. You will have other things that the world seeks. They will just come. Confess this aloud, right where you are:

I confess that I apply God's laws of compensation to my life for good. I am a liberal giver and not stingy. I scatter, yet I increase. I am a giver and not a withholder. I go the extra mile. Therefore I increase my return some 30-, some 60-, and some 100-fold. My returns are in happiness, joy, peace of mind, health, friendship,

*and financial freedom. I am the righteousness of God.
Therefore God is compensating me in the earth. I am
being rewarded here in the earth. In Jesus' name. Amen.*

7

ACCURATE THINKING

Father, I thank You for the special anointing You deposited into my heart to be a gift to Your people to bring them into maturity. Father, I thank You for that special anointing in operation right now. It will work, and it will cause Your people to be more prolific, more productive, more creative, and more successful.

Father, I thank You for this series of studies. It is opening up the eyes of our understanding. It is imparting divine life and light that give us clear, precise direction. I thank You, Father God, that these believers have great vistas of opportunity sitting before them. It is the greatest time of opportunity the earth has ever seen. You are feeding us and preparing us for these opportunities which are coming upon us.

Father, I thank You because we will receive. We will grow stronger. Father, we thank You for the power that gives us ability to achieve favorable results through the authority we have in the name of Jesus. Father, I thank You for the royal opportunity for me to be Your servant and to minister to Your people. I thank You, Father, for that calling. In Jesus' name. Amen.

We are studying accurate thinking. The word *accurate* means "free from error." Accurate thinking is thinking free from error. Accurate thinking is free from the errors resulting from care and worry. It could also be defined as "conforming exactly to the truth or to a particular standard." To achieve accurate thinking, you must do some new things and change some things which are not now accurate.

So accurate spiritual thinking means we conform our thinking into agreement with God's Word. Accurate thinking is thinking in accord with the Word of God.

I beseech you therefore, brethren, by the mercies of God, that ye present your bodies a living sacrifice, holy, acceptable unto God, which is your reasonable service.

And be not conformed to this world, but be ye transformed by the renewing of your mind, that ye may prove what is that good, and acceptable, and perfect, will of God.

Romans 12:1,2

Let's look at this spiritually renewed mind in Romans 12. We all need to be refreshed and reinforced regarding the renewing of the mind. Your spirit man is born-again brand new. But the mind is to be renewed. *Renewed:* "made new again, not born-again brand new, but renewed from whatever it is at that moment."

Be not conformed to this world. Remember, we said accurate thinking must be conformed exactly to the truth. The Word says do not be conformed to this world, but transformed by the renewing of your mind. So the pathway to obtaining accurate thinking is by renewing your mind into conformity with the Word of God — the standard which God has set. Do not be conformed to this world. But be transformed by the renewing of your mind. Then you can prove, discern, decide, and judge what is the good, the acceptable, and the perfect will of God.

Do not be conformed to this world — this age, fashioned after and adapted to its external, superficial customs. But be transformed (changed) by the [entire] renewal of your mind — by its new ideals and its new attitude — so that you may prove [for yourselves] what is the good and acceptable and perfect will of God, even the thing which is good and acceptable and perfect [in His sight for you].

Romans 12:2 AMP

I observe people and groups of people all the time. I meet people from various social groups, people who were brought up in different regions of the country and different levels of society. And I see that we reflect our environment. We are creatures of our environment, so to speak. As we mature and grow older, we take on that particular flavor of our environment. Each person still has a distinct personality. But that personality is flavored by the environment in which he or she grew up.

Conform to the Environment of the Kingdom

Those who grew up in an environment without a lot of teaching and academic excellence have a level of development that is not strong academically, unless they left that environment and became educated. For example, many of the men working on our construction projects (and others all through Dallas) come here from Mexico. They're hard workers and great guys, and we have a beautiful atmosphere on our projects. But some of them only speak Spanish, and there's not much they can do in this country until they learn English. I'm limited down in Mexico until I learn Spanish, and unless they learn to speak English, they are limited here.

A member of our congregation from Mexico has learned English and is teaching us Spanish. He has a super job at the airport. But when he came here 15 years ago, he knew zero English. Now he speaks perfect English, and God has blessed him. But he had to learn this environment in order to get along and be able to achieve the excellence he wants for his family.

I'm sure that you have had to overcome some things in your life, also. Well, it is the same thing in the Kingdom of God. Some adjustments have to be made, once we become citizens of that country. We must learn the way the Kingdom does things, how it operates, and adjust our thinking and lines of communication to operate the way God operates. The more we do this, the higher level of success we will achieve.

We achieve accurate thinking then as we measure up to the Word of God. Then we can fully receive the benefits of the Kingdom of God. So be not conformed to this world, but be transformed — or, as the Greek says, be transfigured — by the renewing of your mind. The Greek word for *transformation* is *metamorphosis*, which is composed of two words meaning "to change form." This is the kind of transformation that takes place in the change of a worm to a butterfly. It is the type of change our minds are to make.

The word *renew* means "to restore, to make something as it was in the beginning." It refers to bringing our minds back to the original state or condition. Our minds originally were not contaminated and corrupted with sin. The original human mind was Adam's. We must change the condition of our minds to be more like the mind Adam had before the fall. He could openly talk with God. He had dominion over all the earth. He could name all living things. He knew good. He did not know evil. He was without sin. Renew your mind.

We renew things. For example, you may get an antique rocking chair or a desk. It may be old and not in its original condition or purity, so you renew or restore that piece of furniture.

Now that our spirit man has been born again, our minds are being washed clean. Our minds are being renewed through God's Word. The amount of accurate thinking or the degree of accuracy is increased as we increasingly measure up and wash our minds with God's Word. We want to make sure we are understood. And, in order to be understood accurately, we want to wash our minds out with the Word of God. In other words, we don't want to be saying things which might be contrary to the principles of the Kingdom of God. We don't want to be cursing, we want to be blessing.

People have thought cursing meant just saying a bad word, but it is much more. Cursing can be everyday words, phrases, or sentences. Cursing is saying something which brings harm. A curse is the opposite of a blessing. Curses are poverty, disease, death, failure, calamities, distresses, problems, trials, and so forth. We don't want to be cursing, we want to be blessing. We want to renew and restore our minds. Be not conformed to this world, but be transformed by the renewing of your mind.

We won't analyze human speech now, but be aware that much of what we say includes curses. I will give just one example. People say this as a happy statement, "I was just tickled to death." But the apostle Paul said this:

> When I was a child, I spake as a child, I understood as a child, I thought as a child: but when I became a man, I put away childish things.
>
> **1 Corinthians 13:11**

When we are spiritual children, we speak as children. But as we become mature adults spiritually, we must put away childish or childlike ways of speaking and behaving.

> . . . The heir, as long as he is a child, differeth nothing from a servant, though he be lord of all.

> Even so we, when we were children, were in bondage
> under the elements of the world:
>
> . . . God sent forth His Son . . . .
>
> . . . That we might receive the adoption of sons.
>
> Wherefore thou art no more a servant, but a son; and
> if a son, then an heir of God through Christ.
>
> Galatians 4:1,3-5,7

The heir who is a child is not different from the servants, **though he be lord of all** (v. 1). The word **sons** here simply shows the relationship. It means grownups who are sons of their Father. **If a son, then an heir through Christ** (v. 7). Our level of maturity determines the degree of success we have through the Word of God.

Learn to Think Upon Good Things

Now we need to look at a well-known scripture. This is a vital verse on the subject of accurate error-free thinking. It describes thinking free from error. It describes thinking conformed exactly to the standard of God's Word, and the benefits it brings.

> Finally, brethren, whatsoever things are true, what-
> soever things are honest, whatsoever things are just,
> whatsoever things are pure, whatsoever things are
> lovely, whatsoever things are of good report; if there
> be any virtue, and if there be any praise, think on
> these things.
>
> Philippians 4:8

We are admonished to think upon the things which are true, honest, just, pure, lovely, and of a good report. If there be any virtue or praise, think on these things. *To think* means "to form in the mind, or to have in the mind." *To think* also can mean "to reflect upon." Reflect upon these things. Let the Word of God continuously be reflected in your mental reasoning realm. Let the Word be reflected and bounced around. Keep seeing the Word and hearing the Word and meditating upon the Word.

Center your thoughts on things of good report. Form a mental picture of them. Have your mind engaged in them. Think upon, and have a view and opinion of things which are honest. Have your mind engaged in thinking upon the things which are just. Reflect upon things which have life-giving substance. Have a mental picture of things which are lovely. Form and keep in your mind things which have praise — praiseworthy things. Let these things be thought upon always.

Let's look at things which are true and honest, based upon Philippians 4:8. *Honest* means "things which are free from error, things which are real, and things which are truthful." Someone who is honest adheres to the facts. He doesn't compromise, he doesn't stray, and he's not lured off the straight path. We must look on things which are error-free. We must look on things which are truthful. We must adhere only to things which are scriptural — in line with what the Bible says.

Your emotions and senses can misguide you and steer you astray. You really can't trust them. You can trust only the Word of God. Your senses can and will be fooled. Ask any instrument-rated pilot. His senses could get him killed, but his instruments give him safe direction.

As an extreme example, consider magicians. They do tricks that fool the senses of their audiences. Your eyes see it, your fingers feel it, your ears hear it. You say, "How can it be?" Well, it's a trick. It's deceitful. It's not really so. Many things in this world can be deceitful. They are like tricks. They are lying vanities.

They that observe lying vanities forsake their own mercy.

Jonah 2:8

Jonah says those who observe or look at lying vanities forsake their own mercy. They lose the thing that would give them the deliverance. We look unto Jesus, the author and finisher of our faith, the One Who always provides a way of escape. We go by what we believe, according to God's Word.

The next item in Philippians 4:8 is that which is *just*. The word *just* means "based on or conforming to fact." A just person has his life and thinking based upon and conformed to the facts. We must think upon things which have their basis in truth. These are things which are pure; things which contain nothing that does not belong. We call these things that do not belong impurities, things that make the substance impure. If something is *pure*, it contains nothing that does not belong. If something hits your mind, and you know it doesn't belong there, reject that thought. Keep your thoughts pure.

Casting down imaginations, and every high thing that exalteth itself against the knowledge of God, and bringing into captivity every thought to the obedience of Christ.

2 Corinthians 10:5

Cast it down if it fails to line up with the Word of God. Cast it down if it's not pure. We don't want to allow our minds to become contaminated by thinking and reflecting upon things which are contaminated and impure. We must always think upon things that are pure, things that are not contaminated.

Then Philippians 4:8 says to think upon things that are lovely, things that are delightful, harmonious with God's Word, and beautiful. It also says to think upon things which have a good report. These are things that are positive. Good things have a good report. With God's Word in your mouth, you have a good report. You are a good report. And we are to think on things with virtue, things which have life-giving substance. If something ministers life to you, that's what you are to think upon.

Christian music contains virtue. Skillfully written songs with the Word of God in them reflect upon our hearts. The more of the Word in a song and the more positive and informing it is, the more it releases and inspires Christ within us. That is virtue added to music. So we want to think upon things which have life-giving substance. The Body of Christ is growing up and maturing. We can look for virtue in whatever we come into contact with.

Another example of virtue is Christian media. Ministers who do not have their acts together with the Word may sound good, look good, and seem good. But they won't survive. Only the Word is going to survive in these last days. Only ministries with virtue in them, the ones who are putting out the truth, will survive and thrive. Think on what they have to say. Some will fade away no matter how big their operations. Only the Word maintains your position of authority. It maintains your position of power. It also maintains your position of having your bills paid.

If something isn't working, it doesn't have any virtue or life-giving substance in it. Discard it, because it is not accurate thinking. People are not getting by with low-level Christianity that used to work a little bit. They are not getting by with those things anymore. I want to tell you something else, you don't get by with touching God's anointed anymore. God has let a lot of things slide, but I tell you what, people don't get by with that now like they used to.

The real reverential fear of God is coming back into His people and coming back into His sanctuaries. People are respecting the ministers of the gospel. They are going to respect the true ministers as they never have before in these last days. It's not the man they pay respect to, but the anointing behind the man. You know, people are going to be more perceptive and discerning of men and women of God. They are going to respect Christ in them. The fear of God is going to be on this earth and upon His people.

> **Touch not mine anointed, and do my prophets no harm.**
> **1 Chronicles 16:22; Psalm 105:15**

The anointing of God is a very special glorious thing. We don't want to come against the anointing of God, nor the works of God. Do not come against the men and women who are putting out the Word of God. God has blessed them. We must let God take care of His own employees. If He needs us to help, He will call us up. Really, He usually does not need us to straighten out His chosen people.

God knows how to talk to His servants, believe me! He knows how to deal with them. They know when they are missing it. They're just like you and me — if they get off into error and start missing it, or if they let sin come into their lives, they're the first ones to recognize that the wages of sin is death. Some servants of God are not around because they got into disobedience and left themselves wide open to the destroyer.

For unto whomsoever much is given, of him shall be much required: and to whom men have committed much, of him they will ask the more.

Luke 12:48

God knows how to handle His people. They are accountable for what they know, as they walk in Him. They must continually walk in the presence of God. So God knows how to take care of His men and women who are putting out the Word. You just pray for them that they will continue to be strong and endure and go on.

Pray for all of God's men and women who are servants. Bless them, and pray for those who are in authority, that you might live a quiet and peaceful life. (1 Tim. 2:1,2.) I've seen people who got off on a tangent and really did harsh things to ministers. Really, I respect what God did in earlier days, but I certainly respect and enjoy more what God is doing today.

Think on those things in Philippians 4:8. Reflect upon them. Reflect upon the Word and the promises of God. You either have your own point of view or you have a *Word's-eye view*. A wise man's eyes are in his head. He is using his senses. A wise man is perceptive and pays attention and is enlightened. **The wise man's eyes are in his head; but the fool walketh in darkness** (Eccl. 2:14).

The foolish person walks in darkness. He doesn't pay attention. He is not in the light. His senses are dull, and he is basically dumb. *Foolish* means "lack of knowledge." It doesn't necessarily mean crazy or retarded. *Foolish* means "lacking in knowledge" or "being simple."

When you can see something, you know where you are going. You have purpose and direction in life.

You understand God's Word. A wise man's eyes are in his head — he has understanding. **Thy word is a lamp unto my feet, and a light unto my path** (Ps. 119:105). The Word gives us illumination and direction. When the Bible says, **A wise man's eyes are in his head,** it's not just talking about the natural eyes but about the capability of comprehending God's wisdom.

The Apostle Paul prayed that the eyes of our understanding would be enlightened. (Eph. 1:18.) If you are a wise man, you have understanding, wisdom, and the mind of Christ. That means God's thoughts, which far supercede man's carnal thoughts, are being put into your mind.

Jesus came to deliver man from failure. He came to recover man from failure and to restore him to success. Once again man would be able to hit the mark. Sin is the missing of the mark. God doesn't want us to sin. He wants us to hit the mark. You hit the mark by walking after the Word of God. You may not understand all there is in the scriptures. But first get one good scripture into your spirit. Put it into practice in your life and watch it start growing. There's nothing more exciting than watching the Word grow in your life. It just keeps giving birth to new fruit.

I knew hardly any messages when I started preaching. I knew only a few when we came to Dallas. But what I knew, I knew that I knew that I knew! Who wants to listen to someone who doesn't even believe what he's preaching?

But I simply started preaching and teaching what I believed, and God kept adding to it. I now have a huge file of notes, pages and pages and pages from hours and hours of study. I go through that study file and am amazed at the amount of spiritual truth and information God has given us here at Word of Faith. In addition, all the other ministers who come bring their particular areas of information.

Also, we want to be accurate, according to God's Word, in judging what ministers are saying. One of those who was bad was Jim Jones. He was not preaching the truth. Unfortunately, he believed what he was saying. He was pitiful. Because he was a preacher totally off the Word, he ended up with people following him to their deaths.

You see, basically, people are looking for leaders. People are looking for someone stronger than they are to help them. Jesus said we're like sheep with a shepherd. Jesus is the Good Shepherd. Not everyone is a leader. There can be generals and other officers lower in rank. But God has His order, not man's. Man's order should be in agreement with God's Word. A wise man's eyes are in his head. The Apostle Paul prayed that the eyes of our understanding would be opened.

One of the most common weaknesses known to man is an idle mind. An idle mind just runs in any direction. That particular word *idle* means "not occupied." *Idle* means "running disconnected so that the power is not used." Do you know any minds that are disconnected? Do you have your mind connected? Proverbs 19:15 says an idle mind shall suffer hunger. A mind that is disconnected or not engaged with thinking upon accurate things shall suffer hunger.

I realize that there is a group of leaders that God is raising up in the Church of Jesus Christ. Some stay at home to work and some are sent to places all over the world. These people know more than just what meets the natural eye. They have the anointing of the Holy Spirit. He is constantly being imparted to them by the many ministries the Church has to learn from today. Really powerful things that are not common to the ordinary cross section of the world should be happening in the lives of those exposed to these restored truths.

Sometimes we don't fully realize just how powerful we Christians are, and just how much of the Word of God we have in us. We believers are called to be leaders. We should all be doing things for the Lord. For example, the Lord sent a couple from our church to Africa to minister. They were powerful. After they returned, the husband spoke once for several hours. When he stopped, he said, "I didn't know I had that much in me."

Meditate on the Word Day and Night

Here's an additional reason why it's important to continually think upon the Word of God day and night. These statistics show you what happens when you receive some information one time only, with no review of it. Research shows that 25 percent of what is heard or read is forgotten within 24 hours. Within 48 hours, 50 percent is forgotten. Within four days, 85 percent is forgotten. Within 16 days, 98 percent is forgotten.

The Holy Spirit wouldn't have told everyone to think on God's Word day and night if He knew they would remember it the first time around. He would have said, "Read it and you have it for life." But He said to meditate therein day and night. (Josh. 1:8.) He said to meditate on His Word, **lest thou forget** (Deut. 4:9). God wants you to think on His Word (scriptures), and think on things that are just, pure, and wholesome (scriptural things).

> Then shall the kingdom of heaven be likened unto ten
> virgins, which took their lamps, and went forth to
> meet the bridegroom.
>
> And five of them were wise, and five were foolish.
> > Matthew 25:1,2

Five of them were wise. We have learned that a
wise man's eyes are in his head, and a wise person is
one who has understanding. These virgins went out
to meet the bridegroom. Five of them were wise and
five were foolish, lacking understanding. The foolish
ones took lamps, but took no oil with them. Oil is
symbolic of truth. They all had lamps, devices with the
capability of producing light when some type of energy
flows through it. In this case, the energy was the oil,
or the Word of truth.

Jesus said, **The words that I speak unto you, they
are spirit, and they are life** (John 6:63). And Hebrews
4:12 says that the Word of God is quick and powerful,
or filled with power. So there were 10 virgins, and all
of them had lamps. Five were wise and had
understanding. Five were foolish and lacked
understanding. They took their lamps but took no oil
with them. We could say they didn't have any
understanding. But the wise ones took oil in their
vessels with their lamps. And while the bridegroom
tarried, they all slumbered and slept.

> And at midnight there was a cry made, Behold, the
> bridegroom cometh; go ye out to meet him.
>
> Then all those virgins arose, and trimmed their lamps.
>
> And the foolish said unto the wise, Give us of your
> oil; for our lamps are gone out.
>
> But the wise answered, saying, Not so; lest there be
> not enough for us and you: but go ye rather to them
> that sell, and buy for yourselves.
> > Matthew 25:6-9

Get to where there is some oil. Get to where there is some understanding. Go to those who are dealing God's commodities and start getting some for yourself. Jesus said, **Buy of me gold tried in the fire** (Rev. 3:18). What is that? That is the Word. Anoint your eyes with oil so you may see. Don't be foolish and get caught with an empty or idle mind. Get some Word working in your life. *If they don't have it where you attend church, then find a place that does have it and go there.* If there is no church like that near you, get cassette tapes and learn from them. *Whatever you have to do, get it.* That's my responsibility to stir you up to get the Word of God.

> And the very God of peace sanctify you wholly; and I pray God your whole spirit and soul and body be preserved blameless unto the coming of our Lord Jesus Christ.
>
>   1 Thessalonians 5:23

That means, may the very God of peace sanctify you, and cleanse or purge you wholly, totally. All of you, all three parts of your being — spirit, soul, and body. John 15 tells us how with a beautiful illustration of how God cleanses us. It shows how our thinking becomes accurate.

> I am the True Vine, and My Father is the Vinedresser.
>
> Any branch in Me that does not bear fruit — that stops bearing — He cuts away (trims off, takes away). And He cleanses and repeatedly prunes every branch that continues to bear fruit, to make it bear more and richer and more excellent fruit.
>
> You are cleansed and pruned already, because of the Word which I have given you — the teachings I have discussed with you.
>
> Dwell in Me and I will dwell in you. — Live in Me and I will live in you. Just as no branch can bear fruit of itself without abiding in (vitally united to) the vine, neither can you bear fruit unless you abide in Me.

I am the Vine, you are the branches. Whoever lives in Me and I in him bears much (abundant) fruit. However, apart from Me — cut off from vital union with Me — you can do nothing.

If you live in Me — abide vitally united to Me — and My words remain in you and continue to live in your hearts, ask whatever you will and it shall be done for you.

John 15:1-5,7 AMP

God purges the branch which bears fruit so it can bring forth more fruit. The third verse of the *King James Version* tells how it is done: **Now ye are clean through the word which I have spoken unto you.** *To purge* means "to cleanse." Every branch in me that does not bear fruit my God takes away, and every branch that bears fruit He purges and cleanses. Fruitless branches are trimmed off and discarded. Fruitful branches are cleansed for even greater productivity. This is like housecleaning or office reorganization for greater efficiency. It's like tuning up your car.

Despise not the chastening (the instructing) **of the Lord; neither be weary of his correction. For whom the Lord loveth he correcteth** (Prov. 3:11,12). God purges and cleanses every branch that is bearing fruit so that it will bring forth more fruit. Then John tells us how to purge. The word *purge* means "to clean" or "to cleanse." We are cleansed or purged through the Word, the washing of the Word of God, the renewing of the mind, the restoring of the mind by God's Word. Not by calamities or trials and tribulations, but by the Word.

The Bible instructs us to despise not the chastening of the Lord. (Heb. 12:5.) Some folks thought that meant breaking us, or sending cancer upon us, but that is not true. Chastening is when God instructs you. God is instructing you through His Word. If you let your mind wander, you shall have an idle mind. An idle mind shall suffer hunger. (Prov. 19:15.) Well, if an idle mind shall suffer hunger, then a mind engaged in thinking upon accurate truths shall not suffer hunger. That mind will be fat. So we must not despise the chastening or the instructions of the Lord. Allow your mind and your thinking to be renewed by listening to what God is saying.

You are a spirit being. God deals with you through words that are spirit. And that is the way you grow. If going through trials and tribulations made you strong, we should be giants. Some Christians have believed in "suffering for Jesus" for years and years and years. But that is unscriptural. Don't misunderstand. There *is* a suffering for Jesus because of the Word of God within you, a persecution for the Word's sake. These increase as you become spiritually stronger. But I'm talking here about misunderstanding this whole subject. If suffering trials and tribulations would have made them strong, these people would be spiritual giants walking the earth today. But I haven't seen too many of them living as spiritual giants. They're the ones who are not getting healed, who don't have the money to pay their bills, while they talk against prospering and getting healed.

If you break the branch off the tree, it withers. That branch draws sap, it draws strength, it draws life from that tree. Jesus is the main part of the tree, and you draw your life and strength from Him. Then you have the strength to bear fruit and to bring forth more fruit.

So the renewing of your mind by the washing of the Word brings you into a position where you'll be more fruitful. Being sanctified wholly by God's pure Word and thinking upon these things brings you into a position where you will be more fruitful. God is well pleased with believers who are fruitful. There are seasons for being fruitful. There is a time to sow and a time to reap. You can't lose patience in between. If you are doing what you're supposed to be doing, God is pleased with you. You will reap and bring forth fruit if you faint not and continue to stand your ground.

We went four and one-half years from the time I was called into the ministry until I started working in that call. Can you imagine Jesus calling you up on the telephone, so to speak, speaking audibly in your heart saying He wants you to preach — then you have to wait more than four years to do it? I'll tell you, that will exercise some patience in you.

There may be a period of time when it looks as if nothing is happening. But if you are continuing to submit yourselves to God's teaching and God's Word, eventually that seed of God's Word will germinate. That little plant is going to push away the obstacles, and it shall reproduce after its kind. It will grow up to be the tree that it was designed to be. Somewhere it will show up. If you keep it watered, it will show up. It may take longer than you think it should. But to everything there is a season, and that is the period between the time you sow and the time you reap.

God is the One Who knows the most about the seasons. We must leave it in His hands. If we will do our part, He will do His part. You may have had premature launchings. You may have blasted out and circled back around and found that you didn't have enough feathers on your wings. You may have had a crash landing and picked up your little old wings and went back home. Most of us have had a desire to serve God, but acted prematurely. But we can get it straightened out right.

> **For ye have need of patience, that, after ye have done the will of God, ye might receive the promise.**
>
> **Hebrews 10:36**

Moses had in his heart what he was supposed to do. His first actions were just a little premature, and he had to go back for 40 years of feeding sheep . . . on the back side of the desert. How do you like the backside of the desert? Do you want to wait 40 years, or any length of time? Well, then, you must do it right the first time.

> **For to be carnally minded is death; but to be spiritually minded is life and peace.**
>
> **Romans 8:6**

> **Now the mind of the flesh [which is sense and reason without the Holy Spirit] is death — death that comprises all the miseries arising from sin, both here and hereafter. But the mind of the (Holy) Spirit is life and soul-peace [both now and forever].**
>
> **Romans 8:6** AMP

To be carnally minded or sense-ruled is death. Thinking on things contrary to the Word of God — things that your senses may be telling you — brings death. To be carnally minded is to be dead. To be spiritually minded — thinking upon spiritual things — ministers life.

Who Is a Double-Minded Man?

James 1 talks about the double-minded man. I used to think this kind of man was one who never could make up his mind, and I found that is the right definition — but not in the way most people think. I found that this kind of man is spiritually minded one minute and carnally minded the next. One day, he says, "Bless

God, I'm more than a conqueror. I can do all things through Christ Jesus Who strengthens me. Hallelujah! Our bills are paid. Hallelujah! We have all the food we need. Hallelujah! The clothes for the kids are coming in. I'm getting that job promotion, hallelujah! The Word of God is working in my life."

The next morning he wakes up with a headache, his wife yells at him, he has a flat on the way to the office and is 5½ minutes late, the time clock doesn't work, and his time card is not there. He says, "Nothing ever works out for me. Just look at my dirty hands from fixing the flat. My head hurts. My pants are falling down," etc.

That's being double-minded.

If any of you lack wisdom, let him ask of God, that giveth to all men liberally, and upbraideth not; and it shall be given him.

But let him ask in faith, nothing wavering. For he that wavereth is like a wave of the sea driven with the wind and tossed.

For let not that man think that he shall receive any thing of the Lord.

James 1:5-7

Don't let that man think he will receive anything from God. He has to walk that walk and talk that talk, day in and day out. Whether or not his little old body feels like it, whether or not his checkbook looks like it, whether or not those tires look like it, he has to walk that walk and speak the Word only.

He will end up bearing fruit, much fruit. The Word of God will purge his life. He will be a vessel of honor, if he hangs in there and does not change his mind. This will happen, if he thinks upon things that are true, honest, just, pure, lovely, of good report, with virtue, with praise.

In addition, he will recover himself out of the snares of the devil. He will judge himself, and he will not die a premature death. He will be a man most blessed in the country and in the city. As he walks and drives down the city street, people will say, "Who is that important person?" They will know it is a man or a woman of God because the Glory of God will be shining and radiating. Hallelujah!

I'll tell you what. It pays to serve God. It pays great dividends. It pays a great compensation of reward. Amen!

8
HOW GOD DIRECTS

Heavenly Father, I thank You for the anointing that abides on Your Word and upon my life to effectively teach Your people and share truths that You are revealing by Your Spirit. Father, I believe we are going to see some things in Your Word that we have not seen before. So Father, I expectantly receive revelation knowledge for myself and for these students of Your Word. Thank you, Father God, for the truths You continually share with us, and for that great table You spread for us here. I thank You for it, in the name of Jesus. Amen.

This chapter looks at how God directs. It is important to understand this. The Holy Spirit moves through your spirit. That's how God speaks to you. Of course, we know that He can speak to us through dreams and visions. He can speak to us through His Word, and He can speak to us through prophecy. He can speak to us through tongues and interpretations, word of knowledge, or word of wisdom. He can speak to us in our hearts, our inner intuitions, or in our conscious minds. God speaks to us in many ways.

Our God is a God of variety. He just doesn't always do things the same way. This keeps us on our toes just listening for that still small voice or just recognizing His presence in our lives. I enjoy the presence of God. I enjoy knowing He is working with me. We are laborers together. I enjoy Him and He enjoys me. We work together. He shows us things to help us be a blessing and to help us be successful. It is exciting being a Christian who knows what it is to be developing in the Word. Aren't you glad you know it's the Word that puts the edge on the sword of the Spirit?

> If the iron be blunt, and he do not whet the edge, then
> must he put to more strength: but wisdom is profitable
> to direct.
>
> Ecclesiastes 10:10

Wisdom is good for direction. As with a sharpened ax, with good understanding, less effort can be applied in your life. You can have greater success. You can get better knowledge out of your Christian walk. I know we are all for more knowledge, aren't we? Amen on less effort. Now, if you just like to sweat and work it out in the arm of the flesh, go right ahead. But when you find out it's so much easier to succeed by walking in the Spirit, you rest there. There is peace. You don't get in a hurry and you don't get anxious.

We have to work to stay there. Don't get me wrong, but once we arrive, we want to stay in that rest with the Lord. We must get into the Lord's rest and say, "Now, Lord, I commit this to You, and I thank You for an inspired thought, and it shall come." It shall come. Things hoped for come to pass when we begin to rest upon the Lord and wait upon Him. He brings them forth.

> According as his divine power hath given unto us all
> things that pertain unto life and godliness, through
> the knowledge of him that hath called us to glory and
> virtue:
>
> Whereby are given unto us exceeding great and
> precious promises: that by these ye might be partakers
> of the divine nature, having escaped the corruption
> that is in the world through lust.
>
> 2 Peter 1:3,4

I probably could teach two or three months just on that one particular passage, for that is a rich scripture. It tells how to partake of the divine nature of God. **According as his divine power hath given unto us all**

things that pertain unto life and godliness. I like that. Life and godliness. The life that now is and the Godlike nature. As we receive Christ, our hearts become like good soil where God can begin to sow His seed — His Word or His will into our lives. We become transfigured. His divine power has been granted unto us.

God has given this to us. God has granted it. He said, "I grant you through My power all things that pertain to life and godliness through the knowledge of Christ, Who called you into His own glory." God has granted unto us exceeding great and precious promises that through these — through the Word and the promises of God — we might be partakers of the divine nature.

The choice of response is yours. Just how much of the nature of God do you want to partake of? That word *partake* means "to take portions of." When you eat, you take portions of the prepared food. You choose how much of each dish you want. And you decide how much of the divine nature of God you choose to take portions of.

God has given us His Word. In it are precious promises so that we can receive portions of the Godlike nature imparted into our recreated spirit. To think that inside this earthen vessel is being deposited and implanted the God-kind of nature, the divine nature, the nature of deity, the royal nature: the nature of the Creator has been deposited or implanted into our recreated spirits — that's exciting. When I meditate upon that, I think about what God has done, and how He has removed from me a stony heart, a heart that was hardened and would not receive the Word.

Then will I sprinkle clean water upon you, and ye shall be clean . . . .

**A new heart also will I give you, and a new spirit will
I put within you: and I will take away the stony heart
out of your flesh, and I will give you an heart of flesh.**
                                         Ezekiel 36:25,26

God uses the washing of the water of the Word
to cleanse us. Jesus Christ's blood cleanses us from all
unrighteousness and from all filthiness and idols. God
shall give us a heart of flesh and take away the
hardened or stony heart. He will give us a tender heart
or good soil. If you recall in Mark 4, where the sower
sows seed, there was the hard or stony soil which didn't
receive the Word of God. So God has taken out the
hardened heart — of those who have been born again
— and He has given us a new heart. We now have a
soft heart, a tender heart, and good soil that is capable
of receiving His Spirit and His Nature.

But first you must be born again. That allows your
spirit to receive the things God has for you. Some
people have a hard time understanding. In fact, it
seems they don't even want to understand. The reason
is that they are not born again or, if they are, the seed
is so dormant and lifeless for lack of water that it will
take a period of time before it will be big enough to
be able to hear. It really hasn't matured enough to hear.
You must be born again in order to receive the things
of God or the understanding of God.

God said He would take out the stony heart and
give us a soft heart. He said He would put His Spirit
within us and cause us to walk in His statutes. Now
this is taking place in the believers of the Body of Christ.
We are growing up and learning how to walk in the
statutes and ordinances of the Will of God. We are
learning how to operate in God's best. I like that phrase:
learning how to operate in God's best. We're learning

how to be successful. We're learning that Christ came to recover us from failure, from missing the mark, and from sin. He came to restore us to success.

Success is attaining the desired end. We are to enjoy the fulfillment which comes when we achieve the end results and win. It takes the power of God to succeed in this life. It took the power of God to succeed when Adam was created as a living spirit being. Adam had the power to rule and reign in the earth. Without that power, it's tough to just make it. But with the power, life is enjoyable, and you have the strength to do what God would have you do through His Word.

God's Creative Ability in Us

Through the precious promises, we partake or take portions of the divine nature. We are born again and given new spirits, our minds are being renewed, and the Word is being sown into our spirits. God has given us His Word which produces knowledge and understanding. He also has given us His creative ability. The creative ability of God has been granted unto us.

Now you say, "Bob, how do we get this creative ability?"

First, God definitely is creative. Wouldn't you agree? And since you have received the Spirit of God into your heart and into your life, then you have the creative Spirit of God within you. The Spirit of God is Christ working with you and in you and through you. So you have the creative ability of God residing in you. You have the power to create. Think about that for a minute. He has granted unto us all things that pertain unto life and godliness. You are creative. You have part of the creative ability of God within you. It's up to you to allow this ability to flow through you.

In fact, I found out something about being creative. The more creative you are, the more creative you will be. The more you listen to the inner voice of the Holy Spirit inside of you, the more you yield to the Spirit of God dealing with you. The more you allow His inspiration to flow through you, the more sensitive you will be to that.

The voice of the Spirit of God is getting clearer every day. In some areas, Marte is much more sensitive than I am in discernment and being able to listen to the voice of her recreated spirit. We've learned over a period of years to work together. I've found that the Spirit of God will begin to deal with me, then I'll talk to her spirit. We bear witness about what the Spirit of God is speaking to us. If we obey it and walk after it, we always succeed. But when we back off and put it on the shelf, in a few days or weeks or months, we say, "Yes, we missed it. Boy, it sure would have turned out better if we had just gone by what the Holy Spirit was telling us to do."

A few mistakes will help you listen a little better. That is not God's best way for you to learn, but you can learn from your mistakes. When you do something wrong, then you can learn not to do it again. God has given us the Bible to instruct us. The Bible is His textbook, and it is full of illustrations of men and women who listened to God and did things right the first time. A few illustrations are of those who failed to do what God told them to do and they missed it. They failed. The Word shows that some backed up, asked God to forgive them, repented, and went on and made it. So we can do that also.

The creative ability of God is released through the tongue. Life and death are in the power of the tongue.

In James, the tongue is compared to a bit guiding a horse or a rudder steering a ship. Like a bit or a rudder, the tongue is little but it can control great things. Your tongue can control your whole life. Isn't that exciting? With your tongue you can release the creative ability of God. You can direct your life. You can be directed by the Word of God and the ability of God within you.

Recently, I talked with a man who had some tough situations in his life. Within just a few minutes of conversation, I heard with his own mouth where he was missing it. He actually had just, so to speak, cut his own throat with his mouth. He was cursing the things he was doing. No wonder things were dying all around him, for he was speaking death to them.

We Are God's Fellow Workers

First Corinthians 3:9 says that we are God's fellow workers. In other words, we are workers together. We work together with God. Confess this aloud now:

I work together with God. I am like God's tilled soil, and God sows His Word, which is Spirit and life, into my heart. Therefore the Word and I work together. God and I work together. The Word is working mightily in me.

That has to make you more powerful than someone who is not born again. You are more powerful than a person who is dead. With God's Word, you can change night into day. We are God's tilled land, God's building, God's habitation. God lives within you. The Word — Christ dwelling within you — causes fruit to come forth.

What? know ye not that your body is the temple of the Holy Ghost which is in you, which ye have of God, and ye are not your own?

For ye are bought with a price: therefore glorify God in your body, and in your spirit, which are God's.

1 Corinthians 6:19,20

Don't you know your body is the temple of the Holy Spirit? Don't you know the Spirit of God dwells within you? The Spirit of God dwells within you so He can work together with you and allow you to enjoy the fulfillment of the Creator.

I am the vine, ye are the branches: He that abideth in me, and I in him, the same bringeth forth much fruit.

John 15:5

What is fruit? It is end results. It's what the farmer goes after. It's why he plants a crop. That farmer is interested in end results, and when he reaps the crop, he has succeeded in what he set out to do.

We used to build houses. I remember we used to get the plans. That's all it would be — just a piece of paper. Plans for 12 houses would come out of a big roll. We would unroll those plans. Among them would be a big "plot plan." That would show where all the houses were to go. It was all just on paper. But soon the sub-contractors would arrive and begin to drive stakes into the ground and put up their strings and corner boards.

Then the plumber would come in and run his measuring tape over the end of the string to find where his pipes and stacks were going to go. Soon after he finished, the foundation crew would come in and put the sand down. Then the steel would arrive, and the concrete would be poured. Next, the walls would be raised. Soon the project would be completed.

The architects or designers had a vision. They hoped to see the finished product. They put their faith in a company. With corresponding actions, they drew up detailed blueprints and specifications. Soon the end results — the completed houses were obtained.

And that's the way our lives are. We've looked at success in planning and how to plan your life and how to have what the Spirit of God inspires in your mind. It's something you have a vision for or hope to achieve. First, you plan it out, then you begin to take the necessary steps of action, corresponding actions of faith to see it fulfilled. You have to believe in what you're doing. You have to believe in your corresponding actions of faith. If you don't believe in your corresponding actions of faith, forget it. Under those conditions, you won't receive what you're acting on.

Lots of people get out of wheelchairs and walk. But just getting out of a wheelchair doesn't make you walk. It takes believing you're going to walk when you get up out of that wheelchair. People throw away their eyeglasses, but that doesn't heal their eyesight. It takes believing, then receiving the physical manifestation. Then throw away your eyeglasses.

I'm laying a foundation here for teaching how God directs. First of all, direction comes from within your spirit man, from within the good soil of a good heart. Meditate on all that 1 Corinthians 1:30 offers you: **But of him are ye in Christ Jesus, who of God is made unto us wisdom, and righteousness, and sanctification, and redemption.**

Jesus has been made unto you wisdom, righteousness or right standing with God, sanctification — through His blood you have been cleansed — and redemption. You have been recovered from a low estate to a high estate, a heavenly estate or a heavenly position in Christ. The implanted Word has been made unto you wisdom. As you know and understand more of the Word, you will receive more direction. As you plant more Word in your heart, you shall receive more direction.

How many Christians lack direction? I'll tell you something, the majority do not have much direction in their lives. Of those Christians that you know, how many have direction and purpose? Very few, I expect. But the more Word you get, the easier it gets to have direction in your life. I know God's direction on healing. I know it's His will for me to live in divine health. I know God's best is not to get healed and lose it. His will is for us to get healed and stay healed.

God's will is not to allow the evil one to ensnare you. Don't be taken captive by Satan at his will. Don't allow the lusts of the flesh or the intense desires of the senses to woo you. Don't let Satan successfully tempt you or lure you. Don't let Satan persuade you to go off course. Don't let him entice you to step out of obedience to God or out of the will of God.

When you know better than to do that, you know the will of God along those lines. Therefore you have direction. You know how God directs. He tells you what you should do. Now that is the overview. And then there is just the nitty-gritty nuts and bolts of everyday life. He will give you leading in this area, too.

Jesus Has Been Made Unto Us Wisdom

Wisdom has been defined as "the sayings of wise men." The whole Bible is full of sayings of wise men. *Wisdom* means "comparing life situations with spiritual truths." That's where the real icing on the cake is, taking spiritual truths and relating them to everyday life situations. Do you know how that happens? It comes from meditating on God's Word. Memorizing a scripture doesn't give you the understanding. You must understand it. And when you understand it, you will know how to apply it to life situations. You could say that in reverse. When you know how to apply scripture to life situations, then you understand it.

> **Roll your works upon the Lord — commit and trust them wholly to Him; [He will cause your thoughts to become agreeable to His will, and] so shall your plans be established and succeed.**
> **Proverbs 16:3 AMP**

I use Proverbs 16:3 every day. I give the problem to God. I say, "Now, God, here it is. We need a solution to this. I need an inspired thought." Roll your works upon the Lord. Commit them to Him. He will cause your thoughts to be in agreement with His will. Your thoughts become your plans, and they will succeed. God gives me inspired thoughts. Sometimes it is in the form of a vision, but I see the answer. It happens because I have followed the Word.

> **Whereby are given unto us exceeding great and precious promises: that by these ye might be partakers of the divine nature . . . .**
> **2 Peter 1:4**

He has given unto us exceedingly great and precious promises. By these promises we are partakers of the divine nature. We take portions of God's nature. I lay hold on that promise. And because of that promise of rolling my work upon the Lord, I partake of God's creative ability, and God gives me the answer. God gives me an inspired thought or a vision which visualizes the answer.

You can pray, "Lord, show me a picture of what it looks like as I am completing this. Show me the steps I took to achieve success."

Do you know God really wants to get involved in helping you, from the small details of life to the major life-changing decisions? From finding a pencil to career planning? He does. I read Proverbs 16:3 in *The Amplified Bible* in Houston back in the mid-1970s. Then I took that scripture and said, "God, I know You called us to be pastors and teachers and, Lord, I need to know where. Lord, I thank You, and I roll onto You this work of building a church."

Then I had a vision about building a church. One night I was lying in bed meditating on the Word and on what God had called me to do. And I saw an asphalt highway. It curved, and then it went a different direction. And right at the end of it, facing me, was a giant oak tree. To the left of the tree was a church building under construction. In my spirit man, this vision was saying to me, "Your ministry is going to change from being an evangelist to being a pastor. Your ministry is going to change because the road is going to change direction."

That oak tree represented a strong ministry. An oak tree is much stronger than other trees. In my spirit man, I saw that I was to build a new church and a new ministry work that would be as strong as a giant oak tree. It would stretch out great branches with a multifaceted ministry. That knowledge came from meditating on the verse in Proverbs.

The Spirit of God told us our church would be built upon two things: the integrity of God's Word and the moving of the Holy Spirit today. When God first spoke to us and instructed us to come to the Dallas area, we were living in Houston. Our home-base church was John Osteen's Lakewood Church where we attended in between trips for evangelistic meetings.

Then several weeks later, the Spirit of God spoke to me, "Go to Farmers Branch, Texas." At that time, Farmers Branch was just a small city, and thousands of acres throughout this particular corner of Dallas were undeveloped. We bought our present property at $2.43 a foot. That's because I did what God told me to do. We bought property that cost us about a million dollars. Today, it's worth many millions. That shows that it does pay to listen to the voice of your spirit and do what God tells you to.

I mentioned in an earlier chapter that the land we were directed to buy was at the capstone of Dallas' development, according to a report I heard on television. About the time we were building our auditorium, I watched a television interview with a financial planner who was discussing Dallas as the last frontier for commercial developments, a man who told of Europeans and Canadians coming into Dallas to invest. At the same time, a member of Word of Faith told me, "I have heard talk about the value of land at LBJ and Stemmons freeways three times in the last several nights." One of those "mentions" came in a conversation he'd had with commercial developers in California. These men had never been to Dallas but were planning to go there soon, and they mentioned the same area.

Well, the Holy Spirit way back in the Houston years directed us to Farmers Branch and to the property at the corner of the LBJ and Stemmons freeways. We bought some buildings at around $3 a foot, and within a couple of years, similar ones were leasing at $8 a foot. I tell you, it pays to serve God! Jesus is made unto us wisdom through His Word, and so the Word leads us.

Proverbs 20:27 says that **the spirit of man is the candle of the Lord.** Our spirit man is the reflector of the Lord's brightness. God reflects Himself off your spirit man which is illuminated by the Lord. God shines Himself through your spirit man. God reflects Himself through you — through your spirit. The spirit of man is the candle, or the lamp, or the reflector, or the illuminator of the Lord. God imparts understanding and inspiration through your spirit man.

God gives information and understanding to our spirit men, charging us with the creative ability of God. Job 32:8 says, **There is a spirit in man: and the inspiration of the Almighty giveth them understanding.** That word *inspiration* can be defined as "the act of inhaling or drawing in." So our spirit man takes in understanding and power from the Spirit of God. Inspiration draws in the things of God and reflects them upon our minds. We then understand them and can begin to act upon them. The Word of God is quick and powerful and sharper than any two-edged sword.

To *meditate* means "to mutter," almost like a cow chewing her cud. As you meditate — chew on and eat that Word — God will begin to inspire you. He will reflect Himself through the Word into your spirit and your heart, giving you that charge of life necessary to see where you're headed.

I see clearly where I'm headed. I know some things I'm believing God for. For example, I happen to believe the Spirit of God wants us to have as large a radio ministry as any of those in the world today. Not just so we can have that many broadcasts, but so we can reach that many people with the Word of God. I'm called to be a fisher of men, to reach Dallas, the nation, and the world. And one of the most effective ways is radio. Two-thirds of all the people in the United States listen to the radio at least three times a day.

One of the ways I am beginning to have that thing hoped for is to see myself having it. I see myself fulfilling the call of God on my life — reaching the city, the nation, and the world for Jesus Christ. I visualize each of the many facets of our ministry accomplishing that goal. As that desire becomes stronger inside me, the Spirit of God will cause that vision to come to pass.

I used this process with our first building which was nothing but a little old junk pile. It was dirty, dusty, had no lights, was full of old television sets and broken fluorescent tubes and old broken two-by-fours. It was ugly. Several of us would walk into it and see that thing as a beautiful auditorium. I said, "John, I see a platform over against that wall." He went out and bought $100 worth of lumber and built it. We saw it in our spirit. We saw an auditorium full of chairs. And we began to build that thing.

We saw people coming from all over the city. We saw, as in Acts 13:44, **almost the whole city came together to hear the word of God.** That is my goal and what I'm called to do. I'm going to be the best of whatever God has called me to do.

Then I found this process would give me not only the success I desire, but the success God desires for me to have. I am fulfilling God's vision. I am fulfilling His hopes and dreams and desires. He has given me the spiritual substance to fulfill the things that He hoped for, so He can succeed in what He created man for.

No wonder He delights when you prosper. No wonder He gets excited and rejoices over you. For He sees that Word, the power of God, that creative ability of God flowing through you. That's what life is all about. It is. A spiritually dead man can't touch what we experience. That's why our light is to be shining. It is not to be hid under a bushel, but set on a hill.

I believe God is putting His stamp on Dallas. He said that this city belongs to Him, and He said, "I have put My mark on it." Word of Faith is a lighthouse to the whole city, the nation, and the world for those who are groping in darkness.

Heavenly Father, we thank You for the life of Christ that is being released through our lives. Father, I thank You that we are having a great time serving You. I thank You that we have Your kind of nature. I thank You that You have given us Your creative ability to create, to bring forth, to be fruitful, to have end results of things hoped for. Father, I thank You that You direct us by our recreated spirit men. You reflect Yourself through us and give us inspired, illuminating thoughts, that You give us thoughts from Your Spirit, that You give us inspiration. I thank You, Father God, that we are born again, that we have passed from death unto life, and that we walk into obedience and out of disobedience.

Father, I confess this aloud:

Jesus Christ is my Lord. He is the vine, and I am the branch. I abide in Him. He abides in me. And I am bringing forth much fruit. End results, the promises of God, are being fulfilled in my life. I am prospering, flourishing, thriving, and living in divine health. I am a giver, because all grace and earthly blessings are abounding toward me.

I speak to my life, I speak to my job, I speak to my family, and I speak success, life — abounding life, the life of God. I will go forth, and fulfill the call of God upon my life. I live in harmony in my home. I do not fight. I am redeemed from fighting. I am a lover. I operate in love. The things that I would have men do to me, I will do to them. I'm a sweetheart, for I have the Spirit of Christ within me. I have a sweet heart, good soil, for the Word of God. I'm happy. I have peace of mind because Jesus is my Lord. Amen and amen.

Praise God!

9

HOW TO OVERCOME FEAR
OF FAILURE

Father, we thank You now for the ministry of Your Word. We become spiritually minded, and we tune in with singleness of purpose in this teaching. Father, let revelation knowledge come forth. Let any areas of misunderstanding be clarified. Father, we thank You that this teaching will cause us to be more successful in what You have already given us through Christ. We thank You for it in Jesus' name. Amen.

Jesus came to earth to recover man from failure and restore us to success. Man was designed originally to be successful. But man failed. He missed the mark. The Lord Jesus Christ came to recover man from failure and to restore us to success. The word *failure* can be defined as "unsuccessful, missing the mark, or failing to perform a duty or an expected action."

You took tests in school as you grew up. You may have even "crammed" or studied extra hard the evening before big tests. There were opportunities for thoughts to come against you and hinder you from doing well on your exams. Even in college entrance exams, fear of failure causes some people with high IQs to do poorly.

Well, the same things happens with God's Word. If we allow fear of failure to attack us, sure enough, those things which we fear will come upon us, and we will fail or miss the mark. But God wants us all to pass. He doesn't want us to fail. He wants to graduate us from glory to glory and from faith to faith. This comes by continually learning how to apply and operate God's Word in our everyday lives.

I'm just like you. I'm a spirit being. I have a soul and live in a body. The same powers of darkness that attack you also try to attack me. The same thoughts of failure that attack you also try to attack me. Line up with God's Word on how to overcome fear of failure or loss. If a person fears or hesitates, then he has already lost. But if you don't have the fear of loss or the fear of failure, then you will continue to go out there and succeed.

Doberman pinschers are big dogs trained to attack. When trainers teach these dogs, they arrange for them to always succeed and never fail. They are trained to attack with no fear, and they know no fear. They don't know failure. They would jump at an elephant because they've never been beaten by anything.

We were failures. We were born in sin because of the sin of our forefathers. This failure consciousness was in our old nature. We are learning how to reckon the old man dead and live above failure consciousness. Satan likes to come along and stir up old thoughts and old memories. He likes to try to cause us to become fearful of not succeeding in the things which are clearly defined in God's Word.

Look at Job. This is a beautiful illustration of a Bible character who failed because of fear:

> **For the thing which I greatly feared is come upon me, and that which I was afraid of is come unto me.**
>
> **I was not in safety, neither had I rest, neither was I quiet; yet trouble came.**
>
> **Job 3:25,26**

Those two verses of scripture really tell a lot. First, Job said, **the thing which I greatly feared is come upon**

me (v. 25). What came upon Job? He lost his health. He lost his family. He lost his financial prosperity, and he lost his position in the community. We have taught on the law of compensation. Everything reproduces after its own kind. It's the law of all laws. **For whatsoever a man soweth, that shall he also reap** (Gal. 6:7).

If you sow to the flesh, you reap corruption. If you sow to the Spirit, you reap life. God's law of compensation is that everything reproduces after its own kind. Since we are established in the laws of life and how they work, we see the source of Job's problem. Job said, "The thing I was afraid of came upon me." Well, that sounds scriptural, doesn't it. The thing that he feared came. For every action, there is a reaction. His fear of certain things was the "action," and the reaction was the coming to pass of what he feared. In other words, *Job opened himself up to the entanglements and snares of Satan.* "The thing which I greatly feared — this fear of loss — is come upon me."

Everything reproduces after its own kind. Job's fear reproduced after its own kind and the results or the harvest was the things being taken away from him. Often when you read the Bible, it will clarify itself. It's the same way when listening to people. If you are developing in discernment, exercising yourself to distinguish between good and evil, you can talk with someone for 10 to 15 minutes and know exactly where they are spiritually. You can discern at least up to your level of spiritual growth. You can tell where a person is by the words of his mouth. For out of the abundance of the heart, we speak.

Job is speaking here out of the abundance of his heart. So fear was in his heart. Now it had to get in there before it could be there, of course. He opened himself up to this thing that he feared, continually dwelling in thought upon it. Finally, it came. It conceived and brought forth his death and loss.

In Job 3:26, he speaks of things happening in his life. He said, **I was not in safety.** I would never say that now. I *am* in safety. **The Lord is my shepherd** (Ps.23:1). I dwell **in the secret place of the most High** (Ps. 91:1). But Job said, **I was not in safety, neither had I rest** (v. 26).

If I'm out of faith, then I'm not in rest. For we enter into the rest of God by faith. Job was not in harmony with the rest that God provides. He was not in harmony with the will of God. Job was fearing the things around him, so he wasn't in safety. He said he wasn't in rest, so evidently he was fearful. There was no rest. There was torment. There was agitation and unrest. He had stress.

All these things were opening Job up for the Word to be choked out. He didn't have a quiet and a peaceful spirit. He had unrest and turmoil and conflict. Then Job said, **Yet trouble came** (v. 26). He told us how it came: He wasn't in safety, he wasn't in the rest of the Lord, and he wasn't quiet. Evidently, Job hadn't cast his care upon the Lord nor was he trusting in the Lord. He was evidently leaning upon his own understanding or what the dictates of the senses were telling him.

Is the same true with you? Are the fears of Job the same as your fears? If you fear things, you are leaving yourself wide open for those things to come back to you. If you cast fear upon the waters, fear is going to come back. And the things that you fear will happen. It's God's law of compensation. The devil knows that. That's why he roams about like a roaring lion, seeking whom he may devour. He knows that you're a powerful creature and that if he can subdue you and cause you to have a power failure, he can cause you to fail.

Trouble also can mean misfortune or unfortunate things. **Yet trouble came.** The world calls it bad luck. But this was not luck or accidental misfortune for Job. He absolutely opened himself up to that trouble. In the first chapter of Job, we're told that Satan came to God about Job. God told Satan, "If you will look, he is in your power."

How could Job be in the power of Satan? Because Job had opened himself up through fear. Job was not operating in love. Perfect love casts out fear. Job was not operating in love. Job was not trusting in God. He was not resting in that safety. If he had been, there would've been no way for Satan to touch Job. I believe there is safety in the Lord. I believe there is rest in Him. I believe we can run unto the Lord. He is like a strong tower. We can find peace and safety Him.

It is scriptural to establish every work with two or more witnesses. Here are two scriptures that support the fact that fear is a trap of the devil but safety lies in the Lord.

> **The name of the Lord is a strong tower: the righteous runneth into it, and is safe.**
>
> **Proverbs 18:10**

> **The fear of man bringeth a snare: but whoso putteth his trust in the Lord shall be safe.**
>
> **Proverbs 29:25**

Fear brings a trap. But whoever trusts in the Lord shall be safe. *To be safe* means "to be secure from threat of danger, harm, or loss." It means "to be free from threatening harm." **Whoso putteth his trust in the Lord**

shall be safe. In other words, they shall be secure from danger, harm, loss, or failure. This is a general principle which applies to all of us. As we place our trust and confidence in God, we are safe. We are overcomers.

The fear of man bringeth a snare, a trap, a lure, or an entanglement. But whoever puts his trust, his faith, or his confidence in the Lord shall be safe — secure from danger, harm, or loss. Confess this aloud:

> *I place my trust and my confidence in the Lord. Therefore I am safe. I am secure from harm, danger, loss, or failure. I am secure in the Lord. As long as I have faith in Him, and the integrity of His Word, and do not doubt His promises, I am secure and safe in the Lord. I can trust in the Lord. He is keeping me. He is my good shepherd. He does not lead me into lack. He leads me into plenty. He leads me beside the still waters where my soul is quiet and I find rest. The Lord is my shepherd. I do not want, or suffer from lack.*

Satan comes in trying to steal that peace, that confidence, and that rest you have in the Lord. As long as you are trusting in God, you'll have power to be successful in the things of God. But when Satan comes in and tries to choke out and quench that power, then you don't have the strength to continue on. The fear of man brings a snare, but those who put their trust in the Lord shall be safe from danger, loss, or harm.

There is no fear in love; but perfect love casteth out fear: because fear hath torment. He that feareth is not made perfect in love (1 John 4:18). I know that Marte, my wife, loves me, and I know that I love her. There is no fear in me, nor in her, of us not being right with each other. There is no fear of her running off or not taking care of the children. My love has cast out all fear of her doing anything bad. And the same is true of her love for me. We love each other, and there is no fear in love. Someone can be mentally tormented because of fear.

We also know that God is not the source of fear. Fear is a spirit not from God that attacks our minds and tries to cause us torment or to take on that fear characteristic. **For God hath not given us the spirit of fear; but of power, and of love, and of a sound mind** (2 Tim. 1:7).

The word *torment* can be defined as "some kind of torture, mental or physical." It is extreme pain, or anguish of mind. It is distress or being sorrowful or depressed or oppressed. Torment can mean being caused to worry or to be harassed by repeated raids on your mind. A spirit of Satan comes around and tosses fiery darts at your mind.

The word *worry* comes from an Anglo-Saxon word meaning "to choke or to strangle." So when Satan's spirit of fear hits your mind, it brings a mental torment. Torment causes unrest and distress and anguish in your mind. It causes you to worry and chokes the life out of the Word that is within you. And the Word gives you the strength to overcome.

The devil knows this and that's why he attacks your mind. And if you don't do anything about these attacks against your mind, then the devil will run over you and you will continually fail in the things God has called you to do. God does not want you to be a failure. He wants you to be successful. But the devil likes to bring fear and thoughts of failure against you. If he can get you to back off, you can forget about winning, because then you won't have the power to go forward and succeed.

Aren't you glad the Word gives you the power to go on? We are learning how to resist the devil. The Word of God is very clear when it says to cast all your care

upon him. He wants to take care of you. So if we try
to hold onto our cares, how in the world can He take
care of us if we're trying to keep them? How can He
solve our problems if we are trying to hang on to those
problems? We have to give them to Him before He can
take care of them.

Casting all your care upon him; for he careth for you.

Be sober, be vigilant; (awake, watchful) **because your
adversary the devil, as a roaring lion, walketh about,
seeking whom he may devour:**

Whom resist stedfast in the faith.

1 Peter 5:7-9

The word *care* in verse 7 comes from a Greek word
conveying the thought of anxiety. So Peter is saying,
"Cast all your anxieties or worries upon Him because
He cares for you. Give them to Him for He cares for
you." Here is exactly what takes place: the Word of God
comes by hearing, and when you hear the truth, you're
set free. You have to have the power to be set free or
you won't overcome. It takes the power of God to overcome the power of Satan. If you think you can do it
in your own strength, forget it. You can't. But Jesus has
given us the solution to the dilemma of overcoming
mental torment, distress, worrying, and cares. Jesus has
come to give us the solution, and that is the integrity
of His Word as seed sown in our hearts, and developed
to maturity in our lives.

The devil knows that with the Word of God growing in our lives we have more power than he has. I like
what a pastor once shared. He said it was like the devil
has a slingshot, and we have a big gun. If someone
comes out with a couple of .45 pistols, that's a lot more
powerful than a slingshot! We have the sword of the

Spirit, which is far superior to any of the carnal attacks of Satan.

The Spirit is much stronger than any of the attacks of Satan. So the Word gives us the power and strength to overcome. We read those promises which say that if we are willing and obedient, we shall eat the good of the land. That ministers strength and power to me.

I am willing. I am not rebellious in the small things God asks me to do. I am willing to do anything God calls me to do, anywhere, at any time, in any type of condition or circumstance. And I don't rebel, and I don't murmur. I do exactly what God calls me to do. I am willing, and I am obedient. That means that I do those things which God asks me to do. Because of that, He said that He causes me to eat the good of the land.

I believe that. I really believe that with all of my life. I believe it, not because of the things which have happened to me nor because of the fat of the land which I have received, but because it's in God's Word and He said it. It is God's Word. And I don't allow Satan to tear down the things God said. I've had opportunities to miss my chance to eat the good of the land. But I continue to confess, *"I eat the good of the land. I eat the fat of the land."*

Why? Because I am doing two things that God asked me to do: be willing and obedient, and hearken unto the voice of His commandments. If I do those things, then God delights in my prosperity because I am obedient to His Word. But there are times when Satan tries to tear that Word down in order to zap me of my strength. As long as I believe and act on the Word, there is power to overcome any lack and any shortage.

The whole world is in a turmoil. Mental distress and torment thrives out there in the world because of high interest rates, inflation, gasoline prices, the price of houses, and the price of cars. Well, I don't let those things affect me. And as a believer, those things should not be affecting you. They shouldn't move you, because we have something greater and more powerful working in our lives, no matter how high prices go. I know God is still able to supply all of our needs according to His riches in glory by Christ Jesus. (Phil. 4:19.)

I don't care how much prices fluctuate. God's Word says in Genesis that He is *El Shaddai*. That means He is more than enough to meet every need. He is the All-Sufficient One. He is the Almighty, the All-Powerful One. That's the way He expressed Himself to Abraham. He said, "Look, I'm going to make a deal with you, and I'm just telling you that I can back up what I say." God has backed up His Word with heaven and with everything the Word stands for in heaven. He has backed up His Word. He says He stands behind it and will make it good. He watches over it to perform it. (Jer. 1:12.)

> The eyes of the Lord run to and fro throughout the whole earth, to shew himself strong in the behalf of them whose heart is perfect toward him.
>
> **2 Chronicles 16:9**

As soon as your heart is **perfect toward him,** or pure, then God can show His strength. But then Satan comes to steal the Word. You're reading the Word right now. Do you know that the devil will come and try to steal that Word which you are reading? You may be a real pushover. I mean, Satan just walks in and takes over. Or you may stick up for your rights and maintain what God gives you. If so, you are getting in there and really growing up.

Some people get the Word in their minds and fail to get it into their spirits:

> The sower soweth the word.
>
> And these are they by the way side, where the word is sown; but when they have heard, Satan cometh immediately, and taketh away the word that was sown in their hearts.
>
> And these are they likewise which are sown on stony ground; who, when they have heard the word, immediately receive it with gladness;
>
> And have no root in themselves, and so endure but for a time: afterward, when affliction or persecution ariseth for the word's sake, immediately they are offended.
>
> And these are they which are sown among thorns; such as hear the word,
>
> And the cares of this world, and the deceitfulness of riches, and the lusts of other things entering in, choke the word, and it becometh unfruitful.
>
> **Mark 4:14-19**

Some people get excited about the Word, but when a little flack comes, you won't see them anywhere. They'll say, "Why, I didn't know it was going to be like this. Wow! I didn't know that all these things would happen. I just started believing in prosperity and, all of a sudden, everything went wrong. I was better off the way I was."

No, you weren't! You had nothing when you started, but at least you got something when you got the truth. Now the devil is trying to take that from you. Don't give him an inch. Don't let him take anything from you. When you find a promise in God's Word, hang in there. The devil is nothing but a liar. He doesn't have an ounce of truth in him. He doesn't have the power to take anything away from you, unless you give it to him.

Cares of this world include worry, distresses and anxieties, and mental torment. Cares include worrying about this, worrying about that, worrying about how this is going to happen, and how that's going to turn out. These other things "enter in." Enter in where? Into where the Word is. They are used by Satan to attack the Word within us, in our hearts. When do they enter in? When we finally come into agreement with those negative doubt-filled thoughts that are contrary to the knowledge of Christ.

If you agree with thoughts contrary to the Word of God, doubt enters in: "Evidently I am sick. I feel sick. I look sick. I must be sick." When you agree with those thoughts contrary to the Word of God, sickness enters in. And the cares of this world bring worry. Worry chokes the Word. Cares strangle the Word. The life and strength and power that gets down into your heart from the Word can be choked out by worry, the Bible says.

Some people never know the difference, because they never got any Word to grow in their hearts! Once the Word starts growing, you can tell the difference. When you start overcoming, you want to hang in there and keep on overcoming. Mark 4:19 says the Word in your heart **becometh unfruitful**. So worrying and allowing cares to come into your life chokes the Word. That's what the devil tries to do.

> **Let no man say when he is tempted, I am tempted of God: for God cannot be tempted with evil, neither tempteth he any man.**
>
> **James 1:13**

To tempt means "to be enticed into evil or into doing wrong." The devil tries to tempt you to do wrong.

Thinking on things contrary to the Word of God would be wrong. Yielding to temptation would be detrimental to your health. It wouldn't be good. James says that no one should say that God is tempting him. Evil is anything not good, anything not healthy for you. The only thing healthy for you is the Word.

God Does Not Test With Evil

Some people still believe that God does some tempting, testing, and trying. They believe that God checks you out. If God is doing any checking out, for sure, He is not doing it with evil. So the only thing left is good. So if God is doing any checking out, He is doing it with good — the good, the acceptable, and the perfect will of God. He is not doing it with sickness, He is doing it with healing. If God is doing any tempting, He is trying to persuade and entice and convince you to prosper. He is trying to convince you to be a success and to deliver you from failure and restore you to being successful. *If God is doing any tempting, testing, or trying, He is not doing it with evil, He is doing it with good.*

Every man is tempted when he is drawn away of his own lusts or intense desires of his senses, or the thoughts that Satan attacks with: **But every man is tempted, when he is drawn away of his own lust, and enticed** (James 1:14). Lust is much more than sexual desire. This is talking about desires of the senses. Those desires can come from your eyes, your ears, your nose, your touch, your feelings. How do those desires come? Well, you don't feel good or things don't look good or circumstances around you look bad.

Satan is shooting those negative thoughts at you, enticing you, tempting you, trying to persuade you to become in agreement with them. Then you'll be out of the will of God, out of God's good protection, and out of His safety. Every man is tempted when he is drawn away of his own lust. Every man is drawn away when he lines up, or allows his thinking to be lined up, with things contrary to the will of God. Remember, the Bible says that when the cares come, they enter in and choke the Word.

The next step moves from the mind to the heart. Lust is conceived inside of us: **Then when lust hath conceived, it bringeth forth sin: and sin, when it is finished, bringeth forth death** (James 1:15). We allow lust to enter into our soul and develop into sin. *Sin* means "the missing of the mark." The devil cons you into saying things that you know don't line up with God's Word and that you know are not the will of God. When you came into agreement with whatever the devil conned you into, then sin is conceived. And it brings forth death, which is the absence of life.

What happened to Adam and Eve in the garden? Satan came and tempted them. He said, "Did God really say that?" He came against the integrity of God's Word. He knows that as long as you are trusting in God's Word and in the integrity of God's Word, he can't touch you. The devil knew there was no way he could enter into the human race and spoil it and contaminate it unless he destroyed the integrity of God's Word. For the devil knows the only way he can get to man is to first get past the Word. *If Satan can't get past the Word, he gets nowhere.*

So he started badgering Eve, "Did God say that? Did God say? Did He really say that? Did God say that?" And once all those thoughts hit her mind, she began to think, "Maybe He didn't say it. Maybe I can eat of that tree, Maybe it really is good to see, to taste. Maybe it will make me smart. Maybe it will." Eve began to yield. Her thoughts came into agreement with Satan's thoughts, not God's thoughts. God said, "Don't do it." But Satan said, "Do it." He conned her into it. He tempted and enticed and persuaded her to partake of that tree of knowledge of good and evil. Adam was with her, and they both partook and died spiritually. They lost life. They lost power.

What was the first thing that happened? They became afraid. A person who is afraid has lost courage. So Adam and Eve lost courage because they began to think on what Satan had said to do. They began to think his thoughts, and worries and distresses came in and choked the life out of the Word. That's what Satan does today. He comes and tries to steal the life out of the Word within you so you won't have the power to succeed. If there is no power to succeed, then you have a power failure, and you fail to accomplish the things God wants you to accomplish.

> **So shall my word be that goeth forth out of my mouth: it shall not return unto me void, but it shall accomplish that which I please, and it shall prosper in the thing whereto I sent it.**
>
> **Isaiah 55:11**

God said that His Word would not return void. In other words, that Word would always bring into existence the things that it was sent to produce. *Healing words will bring healing.* Everything produces after its own kind. The Word does not return void. *Healing scriptures produce healing. Prosperity scriptures will produce prosperity,* if you are sending them out. And the devil knows that if he chokes those words out of your life, stopping you from saying them and acting upon them, then he has you just exactly where he wants you, and he will strangle the life out of the Word. Let me give you some scriptures here on overcoming. These are remedies for failure:

> **Commit thy way unto the Lord; trust also in him; and he shall bring it to pass.**
>
> **Psalm 37:5**

> **Cast thy burden upon the Lord, and he shall sustain thee: he shall never suffer the righteous to be moved.**
>
> **Psalm 55:22**

> **Blessed is the man that trusteth in the Lord, and whose hope the Lord is.**
>
> **For he shall be as a tree planted by the waters, and that spreadeth out her roots by the river, and shall not see when heat cometh, but her leaf shall be green; and shall not be careful in the year of drought, neither shall cease from yielding fruit.**
>
> **Jeremiah 17:7,8**

When the devil starts trying to tell you that you are going to fail and that what you are believing God for is not going to happen, use Psalm 37:5. This is a sword of the Word for certain battles. This is your spiritual weapon. That verse will chop that devil's head off every time. When worries come, cast that care upon the Lord. Cast the burden on the Lord. He will sustain you and give you strength and power to overcome.

Apply Jeremiah 17:7,8 to inflation, depression, and all the devilish things going on today. In the time of drought, the man who trusts in the Lord will not be moved. He **shall not be careful** (v. 8). That is, he shall have no cares. He will have plenty. He **shall not see** (notice) **when heat cometh, but her leaf shall be green**. There will be such plenty and good productivity that a drought is not even noticed. This is the man who trusts in the Lord. Isn't that beautiful?

We will not suffer lack in the year of drought or when things are slim or when things are not very prosperous. We will still make it. Isn't that beautiful? Let me give you a confession for times like that. Say this aloud, right now:

> *I am blessed because I trust in the Lord. My hope is in Him. Therefore I am like a tree planted by the waters. I have spread out my roots next to the river of life. I shall not see when the heat comes. My leaves shall always be green. I shall not be full of cares, mental torment, nor oppression of the mind in the year of drought. Neither shall I cease, nor the Word cease in me from yielding its fruit.*

> *The Word is producing in my life. It is producing fruit. It is producing success. It is producing happiness. It is producing peace of mind. The Word of God is my refuge and my shelter. I trust in the Lord, and everything I do succeeds, flourishes, and thrives because of the Word working in me.*

Now do you know why you should resist fear of failure? It steals the life out of you. Watch when fear comes upon you. It has torment. It chokes out the Word. It removes faith. When fear enters, faith is deprived of its power. It gives Satan a foothold when we worry. It has nothing to do with what we were created to be like. We were not created to worry and have torment. We were created to have peace of mind.

If you are in fear, you can't set others free, for you use your power for your own need to overcome. It causes death or lack of life. It causes sin, the missing of the mark. It puts a barrier between you and God, because fear hath torment, there is no fear in love. Perfect love casts out fear. We are commanded to walk in love. Fear and love won't work together. Fear causes us to be imperfect in love and not fully mature. But if we will stay in love and stay trusting in God, then the

Word will be able to grow up to its complete mature
level.

God didn't give fear to us. If God didn't give it to
us, we don't want it. Through thinking on fear, we lose
our ability to think upon the Word. We cannot be successful, if we allow fear into our lives. Fear stunts our
growth. We don't want our growth to be stunted, do
we? If we yield to fear and torment, we become servants of Satan instead of servants of God. Then we do
what he wants us to do instead of doing what God
wants us to do.

Fear paralyzes us. We then lose our strength to be
motivated or to move. If you have fear, it comes out
of your mouth and brings a snare. The thing that Job
feared came upon him. The law of compensation was
at work. Fear is against the will of God. Fear sets a bad
example. If we say Jesus is Lord, then run around fearing what is going to happen to us, how can Jesus be
Lord? Fear steals our joy. And the joy of the Lord is
our strength.

When we fear, that causes other people to fear. Fear
is contagious. But so is the Word. Fear short-circuits the
power and causes a power failure. Fear is the reciprocal
of faith. It is diametrically opposed to faith, and it takes
faith to please God. Fear is perverted faith. Fear is
anticipation of evil. Faith is anticipation of good.

**A merry heart doeth good like a medicine: but
a broken spirit drieth the bones** (Prov. 17:22). If we are
fearing and allowing mental torment to hit our minds,
then we evidently are not thinking upon the Word of
God day and night — that's all the time — because we
can't think on two things at one time. So have faith,
which is acting on the good, acceptable, and perfect
will of God that you believe.

10

THE POWER OF AGREEMENT

Wherefore he saith, When he ascended up on high, he led captivity captive, and gave gifts unto men.

And he gave some, apostles; and some, prophets; and some, evangelists; and some, pastors and teachers.

Ephesians 4:8,11

God gave apostles, prophets, evangelists, pastors, and teachers as gifts to the Body of Christ. These are called the *five-fold ministry*. Some people called into these offices hold more than one. Why did God give these gifts to men? Scripture answers:

For the perfecting of the saints, for the work of the ministry, for the edifying of the body of Christ:

Till we all come in the unity of the faith, and of the knowledge of the Son of God, unto a perfect man, unto the measure of the stature of the fulness of Christ.

Ephesians 4:12,13

That is why I am here. I am a pastor-teacher. By faith. Look at these scriptures more closely. Verse 12 speaks of the perfecting of the saints or believers. That particular word for perfecting means "to bring into the state of perfection." God gave the Church these five offices to bring it into perfection. There is the word *perfect* and then there is the phrase, *to perfect*. Did you know there is a difference? The perfect person is one who has been perfected. *To perfect* means "to improve, refine, or to bring into final form, to be complete like Jesus."

So God gave this five-fold ministry to bring us into maturity like Christ, so we can do the work of the ministry, to bring us into a condition of being like Jesus. Those offices were given to bring about a perfecting of the saints, or to bring us into a final form or condition, to give us what is needed to bring us into that place of completeness for the work of the ministry.

The work of the ministry is the building up or edifying of the Body of Christ, both numerically and spiritually. Instructors are set in the Body of the Church to bring it into a place of productivity, into a place of maturity, having the complete or final form like Christ. We are to grow to match the ideal standard of the Son of God.

The Amplified Bible says that Jesus is the author (beginner) and finisher of our faith, **[bringing it to maturity and perfection]** (Heb. 12:2). Christ is then our standard, as we are looking unto Jesus. Every one who is perfect will be like their master, Christ. I'm sure everyone realizes certain areas in our lives are not yet perfected. So it is the Word, or the ministry of these gifts ministering the Word, which brings us into this final form.

Some hesitate because the Word forces them to make a commitment. If a person is lazy and doesn't want to make a commitment, then there are opportunities for him to become offended because of the Word. Some people who attend our church go on to become perfected saints, as we are all on the way to becoming perfected, mature saints. Others become offended because of the effort or because of the decisions that the Word forces them to make, and they don't like it. It exposes areas of darkness or error or laziness. And some of them just don't like it. It's too much for them.

A quality group of believers is being raised up today. It's amazing how large that group is. Our church could probably be twice as large as it is now, if the messages had been watered down a little bit. But they haven't been and they aren't going to be. *For those of us called into the five-fold ministry are called by God and not man.* If I compromise that calling, then I have compromised my place with God. I never have and I never will. I am being perfected just like you for I have committed myself to the ministry of the Word, just as you have committed yourself to the ministry of the Word.

Telling it like it is doesn't sit too well with some people. But when it's all over with, it's worth it. For that will bring results in your life. It will put you over. The Word will make you a success, if you let it work in your life. You see, the Word is growing up in the lives of believers. God may be dealing with you in regard to many areas of your life in the next few days, but I believe we cannot despise the chastening or the instructing of the Lord. Do you agree?

We are not illegitimate children. We are not the tares, but the wheat. I'm sure there are a few tares in every church, but those of us who are born again are not illegitimate. We are sons and daughters of God. We are growing up and studying and receiving spiritual food daily. The apostle, prophet, evangelist, pastor, and teacher have been set in the Body to bring it into the unity of the faith, into oneness or a condition of harmony and agreement.

Our lives, lifestyles, attitudes, opinions, and options are being lined up and coming into agreement and harmony with the will of God, as it is in heaven. The power of agreement is at work. Spiritually we are already in agreement and harmony with God, but there also has to be a transfiguring and renewing going on in the mind. *Transformed* is from the same Greek word as *transfigured*. You are transfigured or transformed by the renewing of your mind — thus bringing your thinking, your opinions, your prayer, your divine nature into harmony with God. That's when good things begin to happen!

The more you're in agreement and the more you harmonize with the spirit and will of God, the more power becomes available to you. It is power to do good, power to destroy the works of the devil, power to get well, and power to stay well. Power simply becomes available, when your life is in harmony with God.

> **These are spots** (blemishes) **in your feasts of charity . . . : clouds they are without water, carried about of winds; trees whose fruit withereth, without fruit . . . .**
>
> **These are murmurers, complainers, walking after their own lusts; and their mouth speaketh great swelling words . . . .**
>
> Jude 12,16

Jude talks of clouds without any water in them. There are some people like that. Jude also calls them wandering stars, murmurers, backbiters, complainers. They won't have any part in the blessings of God. But the Word will mature you. It will remove and isolate you from those complainers and murmurers. Jude talks about them as clouds without water. They don't hold any weight. So make sure you don't receive them. Receive the Word. This harmony, **the unity of the faith** (Eph. 4:13), is accomplished by the Word.

> **For we being many are one bread, and one body: for we are all partakers of that one bread.**
>
> **1 Corinthians 10:17**

All scripture is given by inspiration of God, and is profitable for doctrine, for reproof, for correction, for instruction in righteousness:

That the man of God may be perfect, throughly furnished unto all good works.

2 Timothy 3:16,17

Inspiration of God means literally that all scripture is *God-breathed* and full of power. The Word of God is full of power. All scripture aids the man of God in becoming perfect and whole and complete. That man of God has been thoroughly furnished. When a room is furnished, it is equipped and provided with what is needed.

So the ministry gifts provide the Body of Christ — the believers — with what is needed so they can do the work of the ministry to bring this unity and agreement of faith with God. God has sent the five-fold ministry gifts to bring the many believers into unity or into a condition of harmony and agreement with Christ for the teaching of His Word. The Word does it.

We've been looking at unity and agreement. We've got a little bit of a foundation poured here, so to speak, for this unity of the faith, this agreement, this harmony that the five-fold ministry people are bringing us into. Now let's look at Matthew 18:

Verily I say unto you, Whatsoever ye shall bind on earth shall be bound in heaven: and whatsoever ye shall loose on earth shall be loosed in heaven.

Again I say unto you, That if two of you shall agree on earth as touching any thing that they shall ask, it shall be done for them of my Father which is in heaven.

For where two or three are gathered together in my name, there am I in the midst of them.

Matthew 18:18-20

You are here on the earth. The power of binding and loosing is named here. Have you ever had a binding contract? Whatever you bind on earth will be bound in heaven, and whatever you loose on earth will be loosed in heaven. And where do two of you agree? On earth. It shall be done by the Father who is in heaven. We are here on the earth, and God is in heaven. But verse 18 says that if it is loosed on earth, it is loosed in heaven. Who is binding and loosing in heaven? God is. He is talking about two places and about things on earth.

The Amplified Bible explains these verses a little bit clearer, and shows what takes place when you begin to bind or loose things here on the earth.

> Truly, I tell you, whatever you forbid and declare to be improper and unlawful on earth must be what is already forbidden in heaven, and whatever you permit and declare proper and lawful on earth must be already permitted in heaven.

> Again, I tell you, if two of you on earth agree (harmonize together, together make a symphony) about — anything and everything — whatever they shall ask, it will come to pass and be done for them by My Father in heaven.

> For wherever two or three are gathered (drawn together as My followers) in (into) My name, there I AM in the midst of them.
>
> **Matthew 18:18-20 AMP**

What does the unity talked about in verse 20 have to do with the prayer of agreement? Asking. To make it clearer, *to agree* means "to be in harmony with your opinion, your action, and your character." Your opinion is the mind of Christ, your action is your corresponding actions of faith, and your character is your divine nature.

God is in heaven. You are on the earth. We get in agreement down here on the earth with God, Who is in heaven, and that makes power available — the power of agreement. This is the power of agreeing or the power of being in harmony. How many parties does it take to make a contract? At least two parties are involved. How many parties are involved in making a will? There is the one who makes the will and the beneficiary, the one to whom the will is made.

So if any two people agree with and come into harmony with the will or covenant of God, He will bring it to pass. Jesus said, "I am there in the midst where two or more are gathered together." Jesus said, "I am there to see to it that it is carried out." He will see to it that the covenant or agreement or contract is carried out. For He is the mediator, the testator of that contract. The contract must be in agreement with the will of God.

> **And this is the confidence that we have in him, that, if we ask any thing according to his will, he heareth us.**
>
> **1 John 5:14**

If we ask *according* to His will, this verse says. *According to* means "in accord or in agreement with." The Bible is the revealed will of God. It is called the Old Testament and the New Testament.

We know we ought to ask in agreement or in harmony with the will of God. Jesus said, **Thy will be done in earth, as it is in heaven** (Matt. 6:10). So when we come into agreement, we come into harmony with the will of God Who is in Heaven. Here on the earth *we* have the power to bind, and God will bind that in heaven. We have the power to loose, and God will loose that in heaven. Are you starting to see something good there? I am.

We have the petitions we desire of Him. When we are in agreement with the Word. We have a covenant with God. God had a covenant with Abraham. God told Abraham that the land as far as he could see would belong to his descendants who would be as many as the stars in the sky or the sands of the sea. (Gen. 13:14,15.) Abraham's blessings are ours. If you are in Christ, then you are Abraham's seed and an heir according to the promise. (Gal. 3:29.) The promise is the covenant made by God with Abraham. God "cut" a covenant or made a deal with him. He had a legal contract with Abraham, and we have the same contract. When we are in agreement with that legal contract, it becomes available to us.

Matthew 18:18-20 is for us today. Whatever you bind on earth is bound in heaven. A contract or a covenant can be an agreement called a binding agreement. A contract is binding until it has been loosed or relieved. The Bible is a contract. If we will set ourselves to be in agreement with it, it becomes binding. Whatever we bind on earth has been bound in heaven. Whatever we loose here has been loosed in heaven. It takes two to agree or to make a contract. But when two people agree legally, there is a binding contract. There is a covenant.

When you and I agree with God, it sets that covenant into operation. It activates the will, as one can activate a last will and testament here on earth. Ask anything according to His will. Have you read about the ark of the covenant or the ark of the testimony, as it was first called? It was a box in the tabernacle of the Israelites. It held the stone tablets with the 10 Commandments, a sample of manna from the Exodus, and Aaron's rod that budded in Egypt before Pharoah, testimonies of God's dealings with man.

The presence of God Himself would manifest above the ark. It represented power. In other words, it represented God's covenant with man. Once the Philistines stole it from the Israelites. For about 50 years, that ark was off with Israel's enemies. In fact, years before it was brought back, it could have been returned because the children of Israel defeated the Philistines. David was inspired to bring the ark to Jerusalem. He had the right idea, but he did it wrong.

There were some guidelines on how to handle the ark. If it wasn't handled correctly, it would bring death. But if handled correctly, it would bring life and blessing. So David sent some men to bring the ark to Jerusalem. He built a little ox-cart and put the ark on it. But that wasn't according to God's instructions. He had told them how to handle the ark, but they didn't know the Word any more. When the ox pulling the cart stumbled, one of the men touched the ark to steady it, and he died instantly.

The ark represented the will of God. The covenant is like a two-edged sword with a blessing on one side and a curse on the other side. As long as we operate under it in accordance with God's guidelines, we receive the blessings. That man died because it is forbidden to touch the anointing of God. *You don't come against the anointing of God, even trying to straighten it up.* God doesn't need man to straighten Him up. He doesn't need man to straighten up those in the five-fold ministry, either. He says in Psalm 105:15, **Touch not mine anointed, and do my prophets no harm.**

I know a minister locked up in jail, who really missed it. God kept reproving him and reproving him. One day, he ran out of second chances. He kept sinning, sinning, and sinning, and went down the tubes. He was one of the most anointed ministers in the nation. He had the strongest anointing. You wouldn't dream of some of the good things that happened under his ministry. I want you to know that anointing is still here, but the man was disobedient in the way he handled the "ark of the covenant," God's will and His Word.

David was deeply troubled by the man's death and chose to stop right there and find out what was wrong. He sent the ark to a man's house nearby for safe keeping. (1 Chron. 13.) What happened? For three months, that man's household was full of the blessing of the prosperity of God. That man had clean hands. He didn't come against it wrongly. Then David moved the ark correctly the next time. He had the priests and Levites involved sanctify themselves according to the scrolls and brought the ark safely to Jerusalem.

The Word of God, that covenant, will bring prosperity into your house. It will bring blessings, if you will approach it with clean hands and a pure heart. Let's apply the example of moving the ark to today. The Word of God is again coming back to God's people. Man tried to handle it. The devil stole it and kept it away from believers for years. Now it has come back to the Church. You are the temple of God. (1 Cor. 6:19.) You are the tabernacle of God, and He is once again bringing back the ark of the Word, revelation knowledge, our covenant with God, the power of agreement.

If you will touch the Word with respect, handle it with care and reverential fear, it will bring prosperity and blessing to your houses. Someone asked my daughter recently, "Are you rich?"

Amy said, "I don't know. I don't think so."

The girl said, "Well, I hear you live in a nice home."

Amy replied, "Yes. God blessed us with it. It's because we give."

"Well, we give, and we don't get blessed," the little girl said. She had been talking to her parents, and her remarks show that they have the wrong attitude on giving. If they had the right attitude and respected the covenant, they would be blessed. I want you to know that the Word has the power to bless, whenever you activate it. Solomon was the most blessed person ever. Let's look at him for a minute.

God appeared to him in a dream and asked what He should give him. Solomon replied to God in this manner:

> And Solomon said, Thou hast shewed unto thy servant David my father great mercy, according as he walked before thee in truth, and in righteousness, and in uprightness of heart with thee; and thou hast kept for him this great kindness, that thou has given him a son to sit on his throne, as it is this day.
>
> And now, O Lord my God, thou has made thy servant king instead of David my father: and I am but a little child: I know not how to go out or come in.
>
> And thy servant is in the midst of thy people which thou has chosen, a great people, that cannot be numbered nor counted for multitude.
>
> Give therefore thy servant an understanding heart to judge thy people, that I may discern between good and bad: for who is able to judge this thy so great a people?
>
> And the speech pleased the Lord, that Solomon asked this thing.
>
> And God said unto him, Because thou has asked this thing, and hast not asked for thyself long life; neither

> hast asked riches for thyself, nor hast asked the life
> of thine enemies; but hast asked for thyself
> understanding to discern judgment;
>
> Behold, I have done according to thy words: lo, I have
> given thee a wise and an understanding heart; so that
> there was none like thee before thee, neither after thee
> shall any arise like unto thee.
>
> And I have also given thee that which thou has not
> asked, both riches, and honour: so that there shall not
> be any among the kings like unto thee all thy days.
>
> 1 Kings 3:6-13

God can give you a wise and understanding heart. Solomon's request pleased God. Solomon was in agreement with God's personality and His nature. So God added blessings. I'll tell you something. God already has appeared to you. You have a more sure word of prophecy. For today, we have the written word of God. Jesus said, **Ask what ye will, and it shall be done unto you** (John 15:7), and **With God all things are possible** (Matt. 19:26). Now, are *you* greater than all the prophets in the Old Testament?

Jesus said that John the Baptist was greater than any Old Testament prophet, but He also said, **But he that is least in the kingdom of God is greater than he** (Luke 7:28). You are greater than John the Baptist. You are a greater prophet than Solomon, according to the Word. You don't have Solomon's wealth yet. Do you think it's possible to have the wealth of Solomon? Suppose someone like him showed up on the scene? If you'd never met him, how would you judge him?

You ought to think about that. I'm speaking prophetically. Believers are going to get hold of the ark of the covenant in these last days. They're going to find out the covenant they have with God. They're going to find out that if they will pray for wisdom and understanding to be able to help people, God will put riches and honor in their house. I believe we've hardly begun to tap into what God has for us.

We had problems in trying to put a billboard on the LBJ Freeway here in Dallas. We wanted to put up a simple billboard about Jesus Christ loving people and a picture with His arms stretched out. A certain corporation wouldn't allow it. They said it would impose upon or offend the Jewish community. But I said, "It is better to serve God than man." When the deal fell through, I prophesied that we would get it back with a 100-fold return, in Jesus' name.

Shortly after, we rented a huge grain tower on a major interstate highway and painted it as a giant billboard on four sides. It is far bigger than any ordinary billboard and cost a fraction of the first one. It proclaims "JESUS IS LORD" in 10-foot-high letters. God always wins!

I also prophesied that the strongholds of the media in Dallas were broken down. A few weeks later, a radio station opened up to us after earlier refusals. It not only opened up to us, but also to Kenneth Copeland and to Charles Capps.

Agreement Is Necessary for Success

Cooperation is essential for the success of a ministry, and that takes agreement. In Genesis 11, the evil men were in agreement and in one accord. They were of one language and were trying to build a tower to heaven, which the Bible calls the Tower of Babel. Look at the amount of power that gave them. The Word says whatever they could imagine, they could do, because they were in agreement. This scripture speaks of the great power of words and of agreement:

> And the Lord said, Behold, the people is one, and they have one language; and this they begin to do: and now nothing will be restrained from them, which they have imagined to do.
>
> **Genesis 11:6**

Moses stood on a hill overlooking a battle. As long as his hands were up in the air holding a rod, the Israelites prevailed. When his strength began to wane and his hands began to come down, the Israelites started to lose. So they brought a rock for Moses to sit on and Aaron and Hur each held up one of his arms. And the Israelites subdued the enemy. They all got in agreement with Moses. (Exodus 17.)

The power of agreement activates the will of God. Elijah went to the widow when she was making a little meal. He said, "Fix me some food first." She replied, "I don't have much." The prophet said, "Fix me something first, and your meal barrel will never fail, and your cruse of oil will not run dry." (1 Kings 17.) She got in agreement with the anointing on God's Word.

Elisha went to the king of Israel when the enemies were prevailing against Israel once again. The prophet of God represented the anointing in the Old Testament. The prophet said, "Take bows and arrows, and shoot the arrows of the Lord's deliverance." He bent down and put his hand on the king's hand, wrapped his body around him, and helped the king pull the arrows and be able to shoot. They had the power of agreement with the anointing of God. When you come into agreement with the will of God, you can shoot and your enemies will be put to flight. (2 Kings 13.)

Paul helped Silas. Paul and Silas were in agreement. The Lord sent His followers out two by two.

There were Elijah and Elisha, Moses and Aaron, Joshua and Caleb, David and Jonathan, and Paul and Barnabas. The early disciples were all **with one accord** (Acts 2:46.) On the Day of Pentecost (Acts 2), they were all in one place, in one accord, and that's when the power of God was released from heaven.

You know, great comfort and encouragement comes when people are in agreement. It's extremely important to understand that it takes two or more to agree. As you endeavor to be successful in the things God has called you to do, you should have at least one person in agreement with you regarding what you're doing. I mean more than praying the prayer of agreement with you. I mean generally being in agreement with you regarding what you are doing.

Jesus sent the disciples out, then later the 70 followers, two by two. I'm sure they were in great agreement with each other. Of course, we know great strength and power becomes available when our wife or our husband is in agreement with us. Likewise, it is beneficial for another brother or sister in the Lord to be in continuous agreement with what we are believing God to receive or do. I am pleased at the number of churches where believers can find comfort and encouragement as fellow believers stand in agreement with the Word of God.

Suppose you are believing for a raise on your job, or believing for some type of healing in your body or for the salvation of a loved one. What if you attended some church that wasn't in agreement with prosperity or healing or deliverance? How would you find someone to be in agreement with you? Churches teaching the entire Word of God have an atmosphere which encourages releasing agreement to like-minded believers. The force of faith will be in operation. You can find people in agreement with you on what you are believing God for. There is great strength in a body of believers in agreement. They routinely believe God for sound health and for prosperity.

Having agreement partners is extremely important. Strength is available. That is why it is important for us to assemble ourselves together. We must tap into that strength as the days grow shorter until the return of Christ and as evil or tough situations mount up outside in the world. We need so much more to assemble ourselves together during these days. We can draw strength from one another by being in agreement with each other and with the Word of God and by living the overcoming life — living in divine health and succeeding in the things of God.

Jesus said this: **If thou canst believe, all things are possible to him that believeth** (Mark 9:23).

If you can get in agreement with the covenant, our New Testament or New Covenant with God, then nothing will be impossible to you. The power of agreeing with God will move you out of mediocrity into First Place. Be a winner! Dare to be a success with God. God's people are successful people. Be sure you are always one of God's people.

Books by
Robert Tilton

Charting Your Course
By the Dream in Your Heart

God's Laws of Success

Patience and Persistence

Right Thinking for a Better Life

How You Can Win in Adversity

How to Find Your Direction for Success

Without a Vision, You're Sunk!

By Marte Tilton

How You Can Conquer Fear

Available from your local bookstore.

HARRISON HOUSE
P. O. Box 35035
Tulsa, OK 74153

Teaching Tapes by Robert Tilton

1 Harnessing the Human Mind
   T108 (6 tapes) $30.00

2 Simple Solutions to Big
   Problems T114 (6 tapes)   30.00

3 How To Predict Your
   Future T117 (6 tapes)   30.00

4 Climbing the Ladder
   of Success T119 (6 tapes)   30.00

5 How To Develop a Successful
   Image T120 (3 tapes)   15.00

6 As a Man Thinketh In His Heart...
   So Is He T123 (6 tapes)   30.00

7 Success-N-Life — How
   To Have It T229 (4 tapes)   20.00

8 The "V" Factor: World's Most
   Desperate Need T248 (4 tapes)   20.00

Available from your local bookstore.

Harrison House
P. O. Box 35035
Tulsa, OK 74153

Robert Tilton, founder and pastor of the 8,000 member Word of Faith World Outreach Center in Dallas, Texas, and host of Success-N-Life, a daily television and radio Christian talk show, has come to a vital understanding that God desires His people to be achievers in this lifetime.

He has been acknowledged as one of the outstanding Christian communicators of the times, and is eagerly welcomed in assemblies nationwide as a teacher and speaker expounding on God's success principles. You cannot hear Robert Tilton without making a decision, because he challenges you to be all that God created you to be.

Unlimited vision coupled with boundless energy catapulted this dynamic pastor/teacher/author into national prominence as he successfully pioneered the use of modern-day satellite technology to build a network of over 1,700 churches across the North American continent.

To contact Robert Tilton,
write:

Robert Tilton
P. O. Box 819000
Dallas, Texas 75381

*Please include your prayer requests
and comments when you write.*

START

BRAIN CANDY

FINISH!

A Challenging and Fun Maze Book for Kids

ROCKRIDGE PRESS

Answer on page 79

For general information on our other products and services or to obtain technical support, please contact our Customer Care Department within the United States at (866) 744-2665, or outside the United States at (510) 253-0500.

Rockridge Press publishes its books in a variety of electronic and print formats. Some content that appears in print may not be available in electronic books, and vice versa.

Interior and cover design: Creative Giant Inc., Mike Thomas, Chris Dickey, Nate Thomas
Editor: Cathy Hennessy
Illustrated by Mike Thomas, Wolfe Hanson, Craig Rousseau

ISBN: 978-1-64611-851-9
R0

Introduction

START

This book is packed with fun mazes to do! Get through Saturn's rings, navigate a messy room, help a superhero rescue a cat from a tree, and so much more.

These mazes aren't just fun to do, they help you too! Completing mazes will add to your skills for solving visual problems, improve your ability to carefully draw lines, and help you gain patience and persistence with figuring out something that seems tricky at first!

Here are some tips to help you out:

Tips

 There are a few types of mazes in here. They are different sizes and shapes, and they get harder further into the book. For most you just need to avoid obstacles; but in a few you need to make sure to collect objects in the paths. There might be more than one way to get to the FINISH, but only one correct path—one where you've finish a task given in the instructions. So make sure to read the instructions on each page before you start!

Any special instructions that you need to know **will be in a** yellow box **like this!**

 Some of the mazes are 3-D mazes! They'll be marked at the top of each page with this symbol: **3-D!**

In a 3-D maze, you may have to go over or under the path, crossing lines you've already made. So take a close look at the paths and try to picture them in 3 dimensions, to tell when you can and can't go over or under a path. Here are two examples:

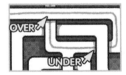 

 Remember this…on all of the mazes, you can NEVER go right through a black line!

If you get stuck, take a break and come back to the maze later. When all else fails, there are answers in the back of the book.

Once you finish the book, not only will you be a better problem solver, you'll also start to see mazes everywhere! Getting through the grocery store, reaching your table in the cafeteria, looking at a painting. Mazes are everywhere!

Now that you know all you need to know, are you ready to take on this maze book? You'll do a-maze-ing!

FINISH!

The Finish Line!

Find your way through the city to get this runner to the marathon's finish line.

CITY MARATHON

START

PRIVATE PROPERTY

STOP

KEEP OFF THE GRASS

FINISH!

A-moose-ing Friends

Help this chipmunk run around his moose friend's antlers.

START

FINISH!

3

The Amazing Spider-Maze!

Can you get this spider to the other side of its web in time for lunch?

START

FINISH!

Any Kitties Want Snacks?

Help this hungry kitty find her snacks!

START

WATER

FINISH!

Trash Day

Drive the recycling truck to the recycling center.

You need to pick up every bin along your route!

START

FINISH!

8-Dimensional!

Swim through the octopus's many tentacles.

START

FINISH!

Gridiron Glory

Can this football player weave his way into the end zone?
Watch out for the other team!

START

Answer on page 80   TOUCHDOWN!

Yard Work!

Get this lawn mowed before it gets too hot outside!

Make sure to get ALL of
those tall patches of grass!

START

FINISH!

Why Did this Chicken Cross the Road?

Help the chicken cross the interstate to get to her coop! Look both ways!

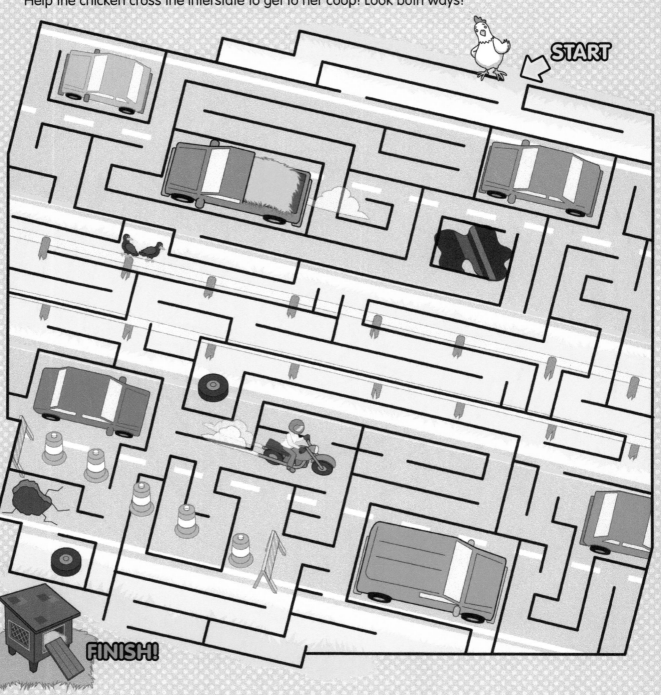

START

FINISH!

I Mustache You a Question

Navigate your way through this fancy mustache!

START

FINISH!

Hog-Hedge!

Help this hedgehog navigate the hedge maze to get to his breakfast!

START

FINISH!

A Cowboy Ain't Nuthin' without His Horse!

Get this cowboy back to his missing horse, so they can ride into the sunset!

FINISH!

START →

Swimming with a Porpoise!

Help this lost porpoise return to its pod.

START

FINISH!

Answer on page 81

Right on Target!

Shoot the arrow through the air and into the middle of the bullseye.

START

FINISH!

Answer on page 81 15

Do the Wave!

There's a sale on fun! Complete the crazy tube-man maze.

START

Answer on page 81

FINISH!

Dig-Dog!

Help Fifi find her buried bone!

START

FINISH!

That's What Heroes Do!

Oh no! Marylou's cat Chester got stuck in a tree! Thankfully, Captain Heroic is here to save the day!

Find your way to Chester, and then take him back down to the ground!

START

FINISH!

18   Answer on page 81

Going for Gold!

Can you make it to the bottom of the mountain to win a gold medal?

START

FINISH!

Answer on page 82

Aw, Shucks!

Complete the corn maze, and make sure you don't get lost!
When you're done, grab a cold cup of apple cider.

START

CIDER

FINISH!

An Empire State of Mind

Get all the way to the top of the Empire State Building to look out on the New York City skyline!

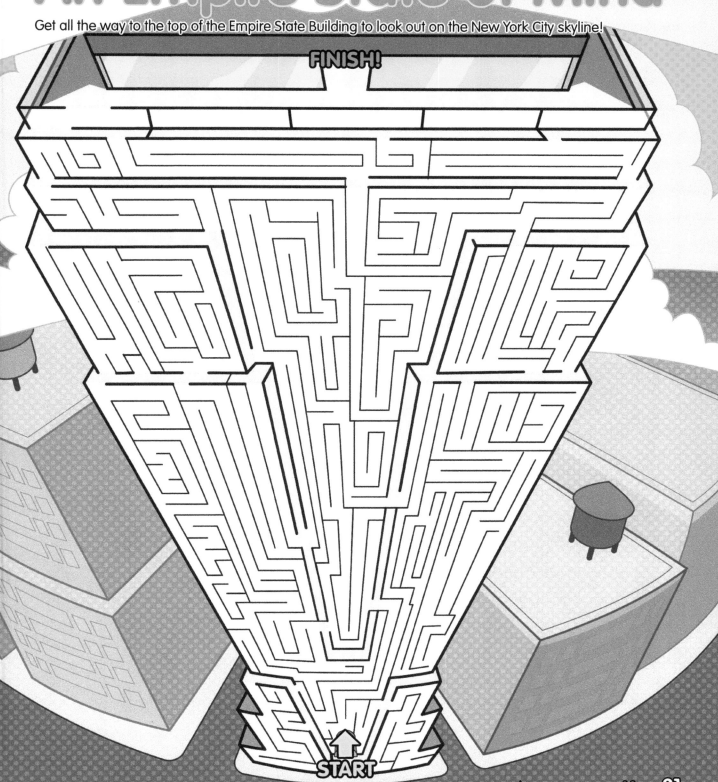

FINISH!

START

Parking Problems

Hmmm...where did we park the car? Make your way through the parking lot chaos and get ready to hit the road.

START

FINISH!

UFO Sighting!

Make your way through this Unidentified Flying Object, while avoiding Unknown Fun Obstacles!

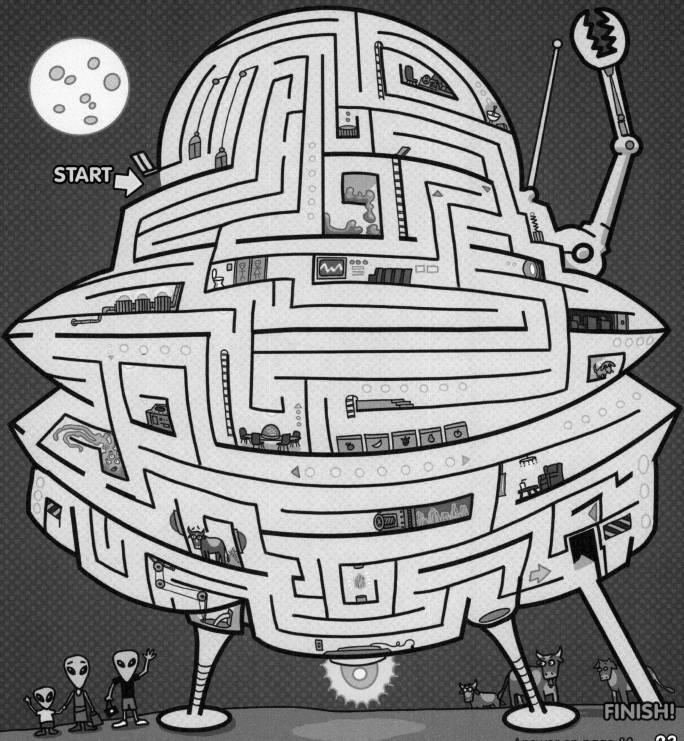

START →

FINISH!

Answer on page 82

23

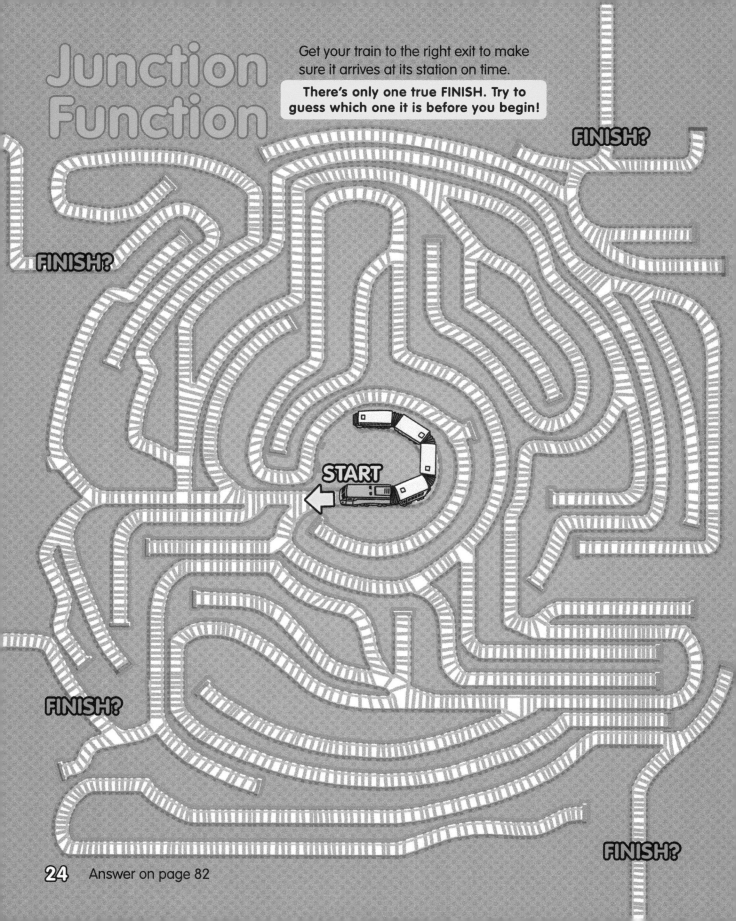

Junction Function

Get your train to the right exit to make sure it arrives at its station on time.

There's only one true FINISH. Try to guess which one it is before you begin!

FINISH?

FINISH?

FINISH?

FINISH?

FINISH?

START

Smiley!

Help Nora find her lost stuffed shark so she can go to bed!

START

FINISH!

Leaf Peeper

Make your way across this autumn leaf without taking a fall!

Answer on page 83

Bee-autiful!

Help the bee get to the middle of the flower so it can take pollen back to its hive!

START

FINISH!

Deep Dive!

Find the sunken treasure using your mini-submarine!

START

FINISH!

Fire Up Those Brains!

Your neurons are firing! Get from one side of the brain to the other!

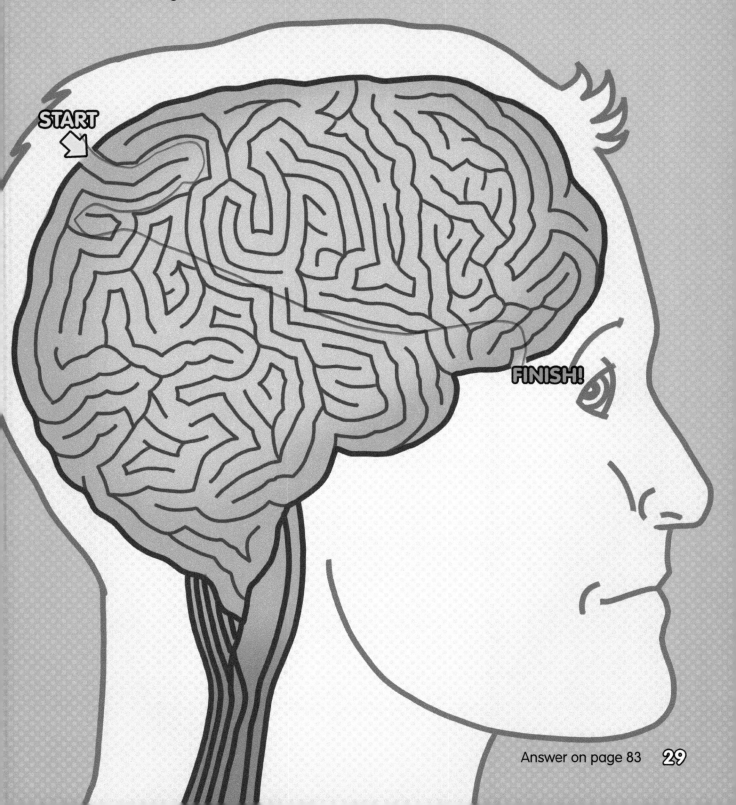

START

FINISH!

Answer on page 83

Beep Boop Beep!

Get through the robot's wires and bolts to the other side.

START

FINISH!

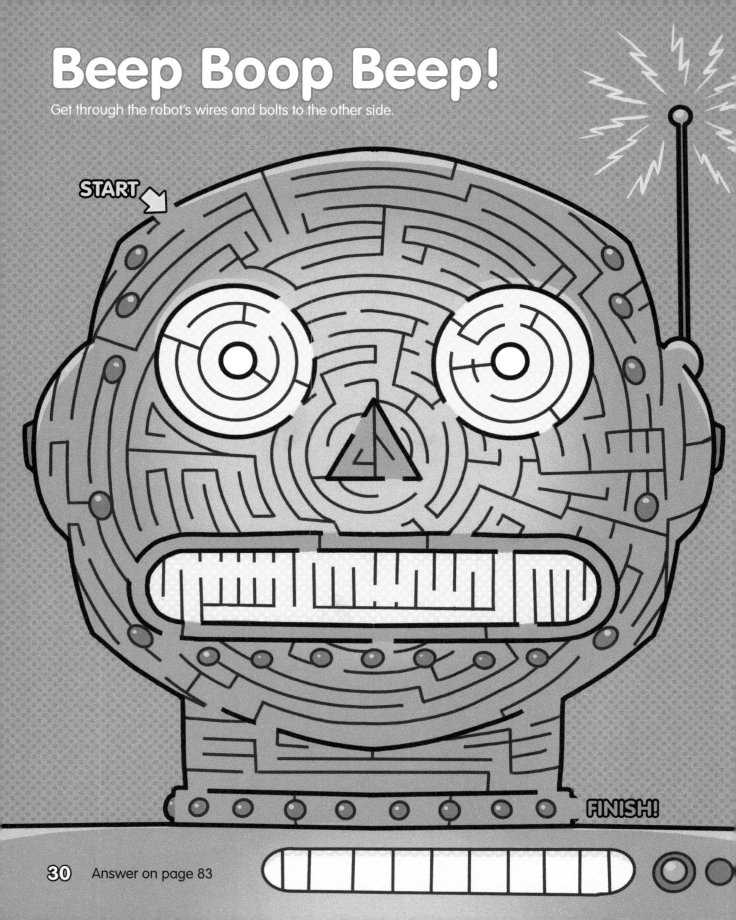

This Maze Is Cheesy

Get the mouse to the cheese without being caught by Bruno the Cat!

START

FINISH!

A Perfect Game

Hit all 10 pins to get a strike!

START

FINISH!

32   Answer on page 84

Concrete Jungle

Help this adventurous cat hop around the rooftops to get to his favorite shop!

Stay on the white paths!

START

FRESH FISH

FLORIST

FINISH!

Saturn's Rings

Guide your spacecraft through Saturn's rings to get into orbit around the planet!

FINISH!

START

The Haunted Mansion

Get out the door of the haunted mansion before the ghosts come out!

START

FINISH!

Answer on page 84

Dog Gone!

Theodore the sheepdog is lost.
Help him get back home safely while **avoiding** mean cats!

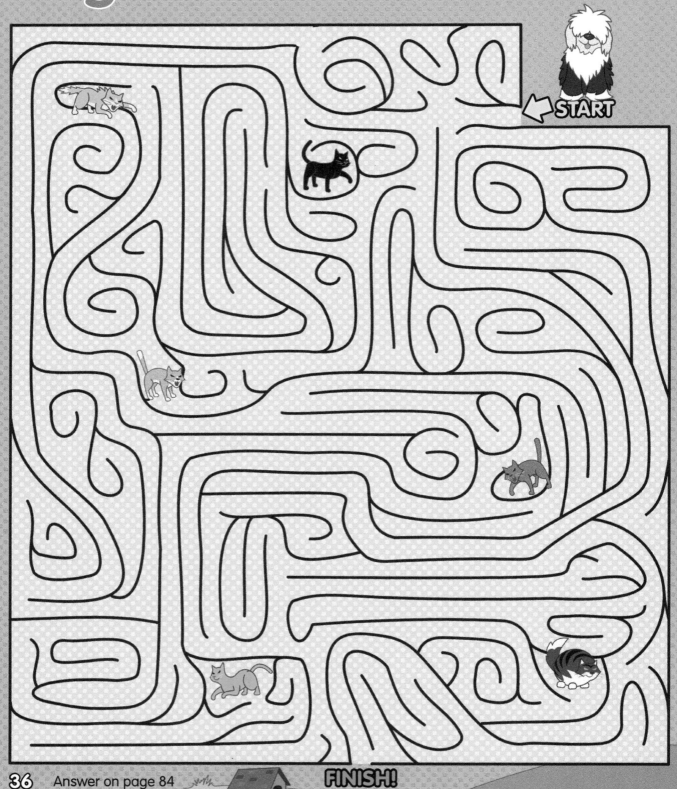

START

FINISH!

Can You Dig It?

Help these archeologists uncover the secrets of this lost civilization!

Stay on the white paths!

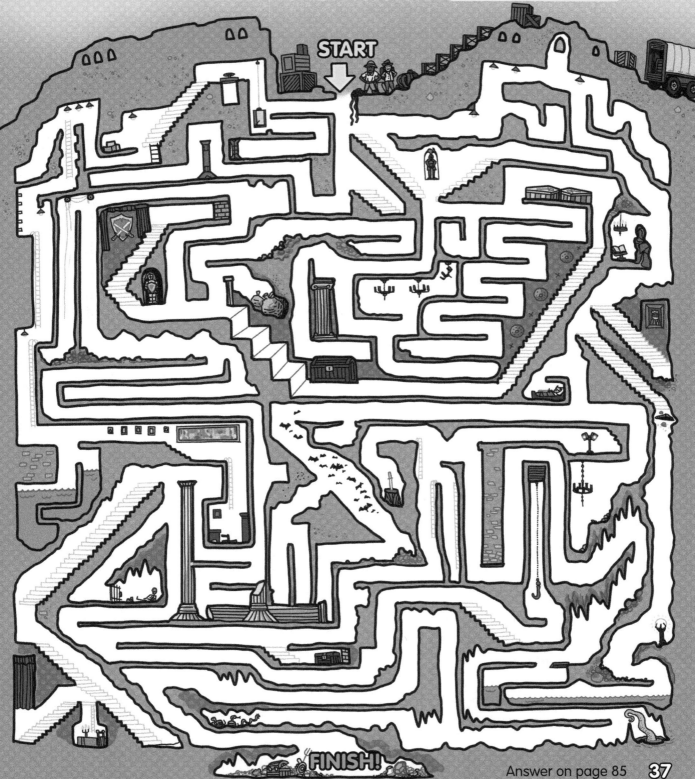

START

FINISH!

Answer on page 85

GOAAAAAAAL!

Get around the defenders and score a goal for your team!

START

GOAAAAAAAL!

Really HOT Chocolate!

Get through the hot chocolate's steam while waiting for it to cool down.

START

FINISH!

Into the Storm!

Pilot your Hurricane Hunter aircraft into the eye of the storm!

START

FINISH!

Hoppin' Mad

Help this frog return to its favorite lily pad, and grab some dinner along the way!

You need to get 3 bugs on your way to the FINISH!

START

FINISH!

Deep Thoughts

Can you think as hard as the Thinker?
Do you think you can finish this maze?
We think you can!

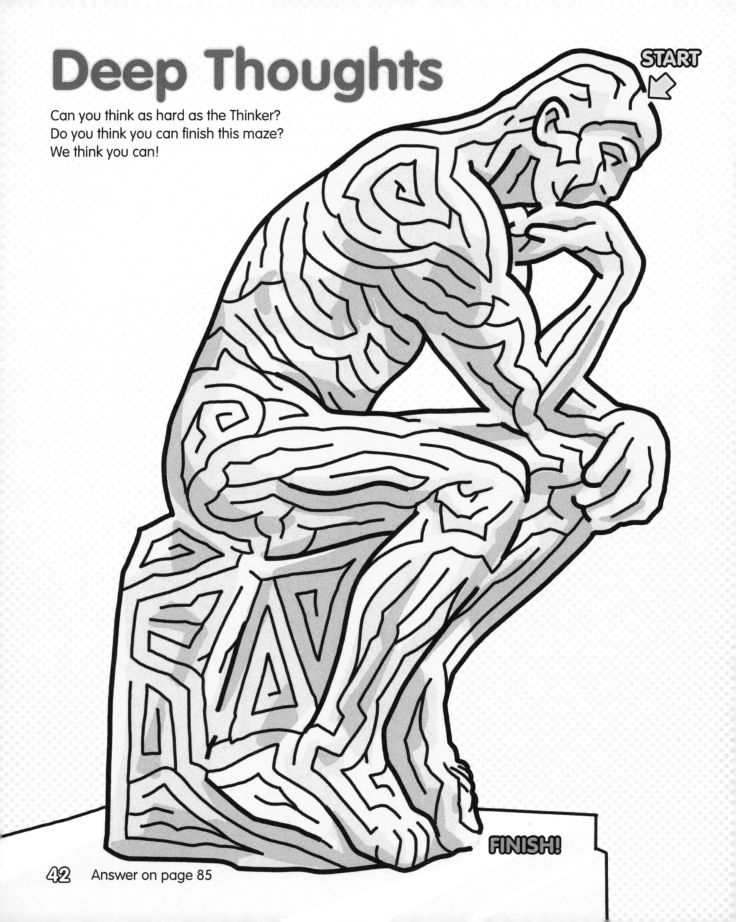

START

FINISH!

Cleared for Landing

There's some crazy weather out there! Land your plane safely.

START

FINISH!

School's Out

Return a library book on your walk home from school.

Get to the LIBRARY before the FINISH. No going back on a path you've already gone down!

BANK

DINER

HOTEL

USED CARS

LIBRARY

FINISH!

GAS

PIZZA

SCHOOL START

Answer on page 86

Omnomnom!

Get your fruit on! Make your wormy way through this delicious apple.

FINISH!

START

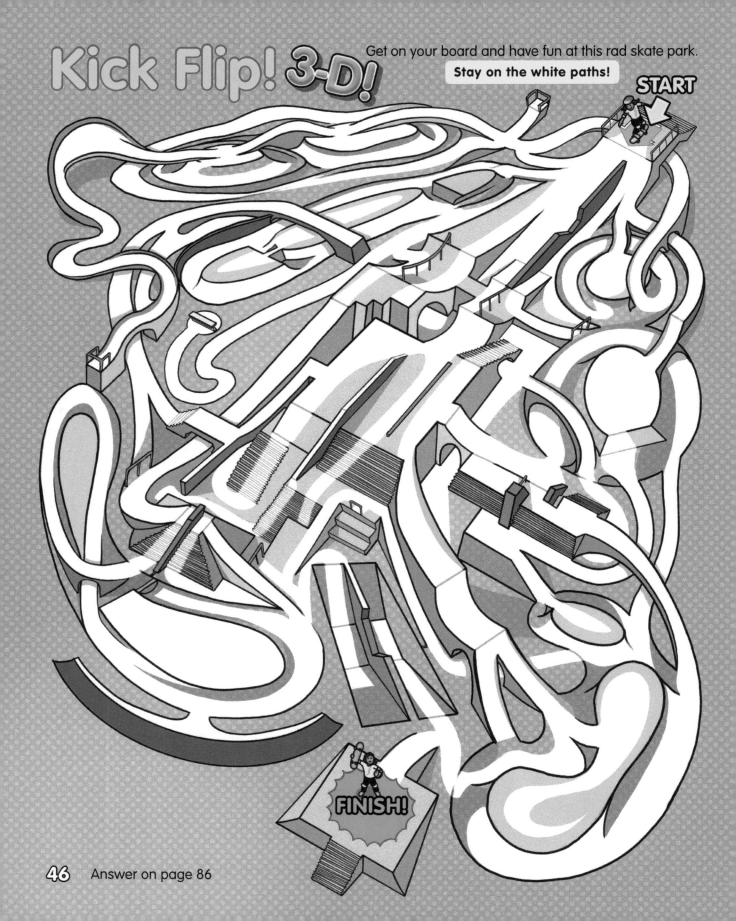

Kick Flip! 3-D!

Get on your board and have fun at this rad skate park.

Stay on the white paths!

START

FINISH!

Answer on page 86

The Most Import-*ant* Meal of the Day!

Help this ant get his food back to his hill in time for breakfast.

START

FINISH!

Pangolin Puzzle

Get through this pangolin maze, then help him get some dinner!

START

FINISH!

Tongue-Tied!
3-D!

Grub time! Help the pangolin find a meal using his tongue to get through this ant hill.

Pick up 8 ants by the time you reach the FINISH!

START

FINISH!

Johnny Appleseed

Help Johnny plant apple trees during his travels across early America!

START

FINISH!

Journey to the Center of the Earth!

What could possibly be below the Earth's surface? Could there be vast worlds that we never knew existed? Help the team of adventurers get to the center of the Earth to discover unknown worlds.

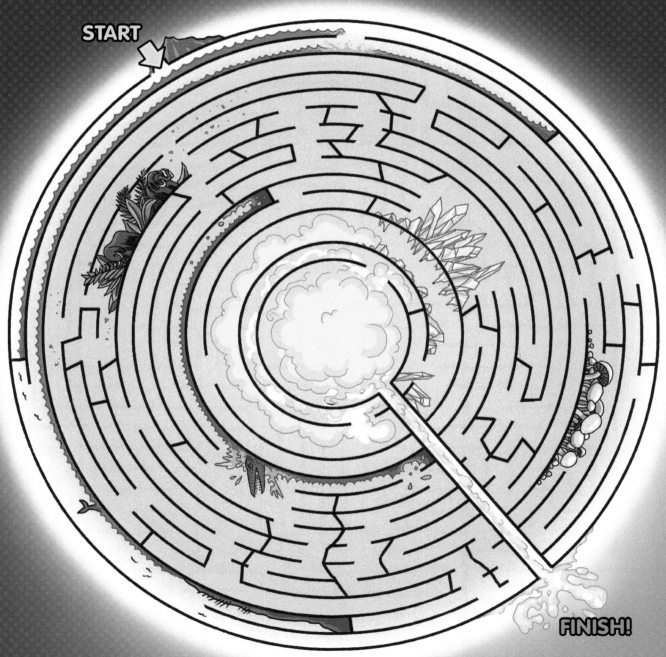

START

FINISH!

Answer on page 87

South for the Winter

Show these Canada geese where to fly to stay warm for the winter. Look out for wind gusts!

START

FINISH!

Modern Art!

Make your way through this modern art masterpiece!

START

FINISH!

MAZE IN LAVENDER
PAUL JACKSON
1953

Answer on page 87   53

Are You My Mummy?

In this ancient maze of the pharaohs, get from one end of the mummy to the other!

START

FINISH!

Serious Blockage!

Get through the criss-crossing pipes to your final destination...the sewer!

START

FINISH!

Answer on page 88 **55**

Hole-in-One! 3-D!

Aim and putt! Can you get through, over, and around the obstacles to sink the ball in one try? Stay out of the water hazards.

START

FINISH!

Meerkat's Memory

Help this wandering meerkat remember how to get back to his mob!

You can travel through the tunnels to get there!

START

FINISH!

Space Invaders!

You can only pass through 3 alien ships!

Get your rocket to Moon Base Gamma, avoiding the alien armada in your way! Your shields can only protect you for a while.

FINISH!

START

Getting Nervous?

Can you wiggle your toes? Follow the nervous system from the brain to the right foot and find out!

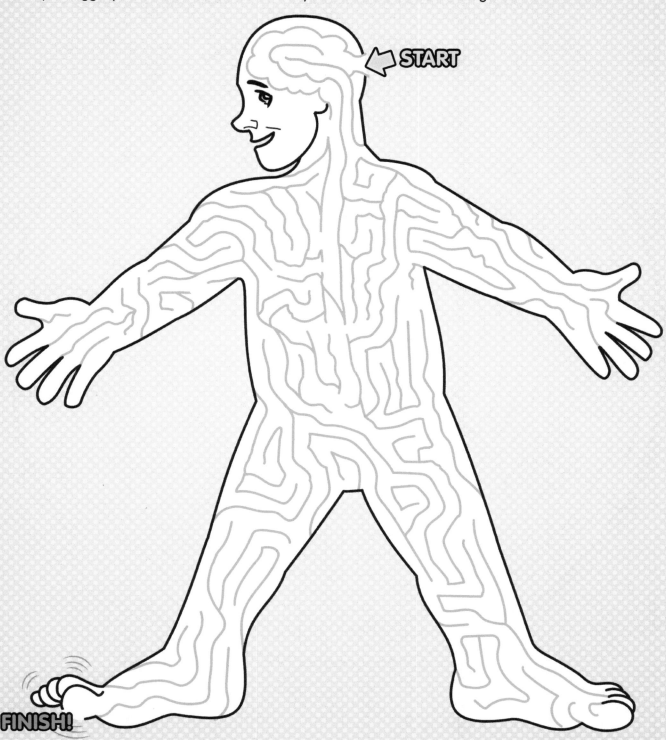

START

FINISH!

Pizza Party!

Eat your way across this pizza! **Avoid all of the pineapple!** Gross!

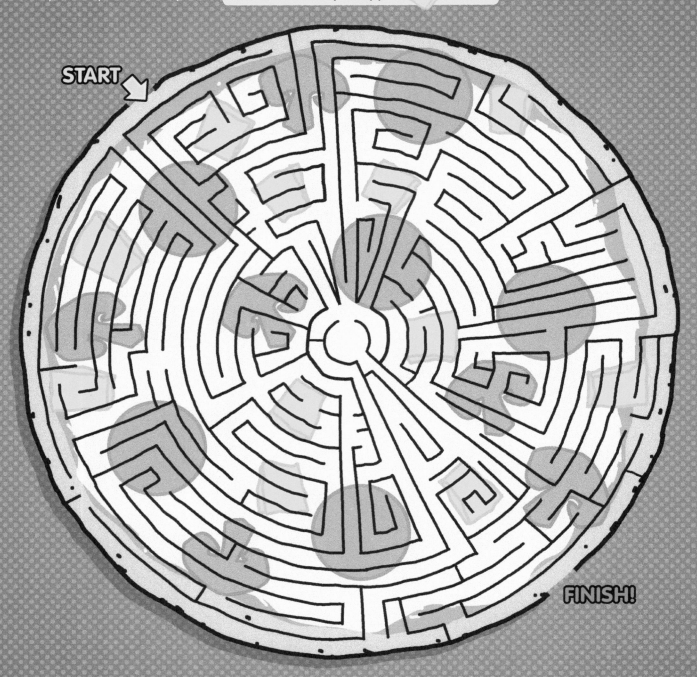

START

FINISH!

Time to Hit the Hay!

Get this farmer get back to the barn. Don't run over the fruits and vegetables!

Make sure you visit all 4 fields before you reach the FINISH!

START

FINISH!

Movie Night

Make your way through this giant-sized bucket of popcorn before you get to the end of the movie!

START

Answer on page 89 FINISH!

A-maze-ing Graffiti!

Can you get all the way through this cool wall mural?

START

FINISH!

Mama Bird

Help this bird feed her hungry babies!

Get to the worm, and then make your way back up to the nest.

START

FINISH!

Adventure Time!

Get through the jungle safely! Find the right bridge to cross the river, and look out for dangerous animals!

START

FINISH!

Sea Monsters!

Ahoy, Captain! Sail your ship through the dangerous waters safely.

START

FINISH!

Space Walk!

You've made your repairs! Now make your way across the International Space Station and get to the airlock. The clock is ticking!

START

FINISH!

It's Ready to Blow!

Follow the path of the lava from deep under the earth, up, and out of the exploding volcano!

FINISH!

START

First, you'll have to decide which path upward you're going to take!

Answer on page 90

Maze-a-saurus Rex!

Can you get through this Jurassic puzzle?

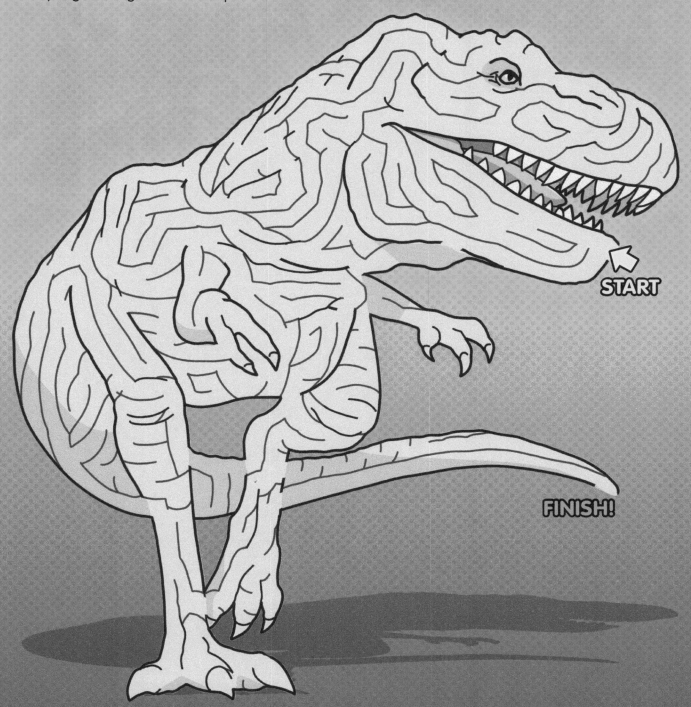

START

FINISH!

Fun at the Water Park!

Help Sarah choose the right water slide to get to the pool with her friends! Can you guess which of the four is right before you begin?

3-D!

START

ATLANTIS ATTACKS

FINISH!

Mazes & Monsters

You can't cast a spell to get rid of these monsters without your magic wand! Find it!

START

FINISH!

Helicopter Trip

Take a tour above the city on this helicopter sightseeing trip!

START

FINISH!

H

H

Moooooooooove It

Help the hungry water buffalo get to her favorite patch of grass.

START

FINISH!

The Yellow Brick Road

Help Dorothy find her way from Munchkinland to the Emerald City of Oz!

FINISH!

START

A Night at the Museum

Are you sneaky enough to be a master thief?

Get to the Crown Jewels, and then out through the skylight!

FINISH!

CROWN JEWELS

MUSEUM

START

A Knight to Remember!

Sneak into the castle, rescue the prince, and defeat the dragon! All in a knight's day!

THE PRINCE!

START

FINISH!

Answer on page 91

Clean. Your. Room!

Nathan forgot to clean his room…for about a year. Now he needs help getting to his bed!

START

FINISH!

Reef Races!

3-D!

Get your fish from the top of the coral reef to its home at the bottom.
Stay on the white paths, and avoid the eels. Don't get eaten!

START

FINISH!

Answer on page 91

Answers ⬇

Title page:
BRAIN CANDY

Page 2:
The Finish Line!

Page 3:
A-moose-ing Friends

Page 4:
The Amazing Spider-Maze!

Page 5:
Any Kitties Want Snacks?

Page 6:
Trash Day

Answers

Page 7:
8-Dimensional!

Page 8:
Gridiron Glory

Page 9:
Yard Work!

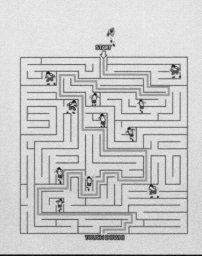

Page 10:
Why Did this Chicken Cross the Road?

Page 11:
I Mustache You a Question

Page 12:
Hog-Hedge!

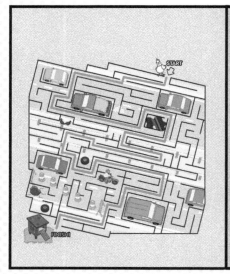

Answers

Page 13:
A Cowboy Ain't Nuthin'
without His Horse!

Page 14:
Swimming with a Porpoise!

Page 15:
Right on Target!

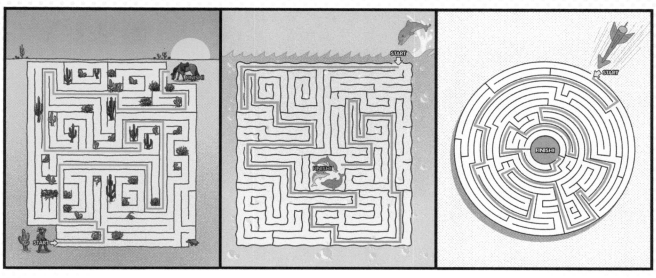

Page 16:
Do the Wave!

Page 17:
Dig Dog!

Page 18:
That's What Heroes Do!

Answers ⬇

Page 19:
Going for Gold!

Page 20:
Aw, Shucks!

Page 21:
An Empire State of Mind

Page 22:
Parking Problems

Page 23:
UFO Sighting!

Page 24:
Junction Function

Answers ⬇

Page 25:
Smiley!

Page 26:
Leaf Peeper

Page 27:
Bee-autiful!

Page 28:
Deep Dive!

Page 29:
Fire Up Those Brains!

Page 30:
Beep Boop Beep!

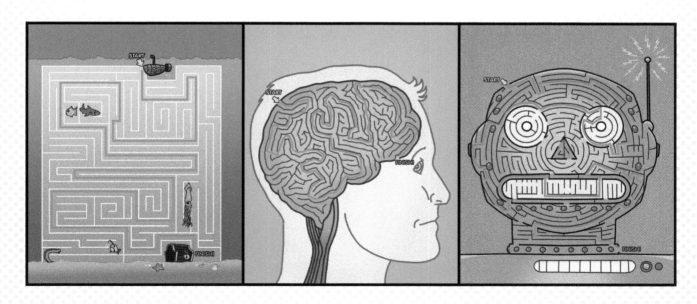

Answers

Page 31:
This Maze Is Cheesy

Page 32:
A Perfect Game

Page 33:
Concrete Jungle

Page 34:
Saturn's Rings

Page 35:
The Haunted Mansion

Page 36:
Dog Gone!

Answers

Page 37:
Can You Dig It?

Page 38:
GOAAAAAAAL!

Page 39:
Really HOT Chocolate!

Page 40:
Into the Storm!

Page 41:
Hoppin' Mad

Page 42:
Deep Thoughts

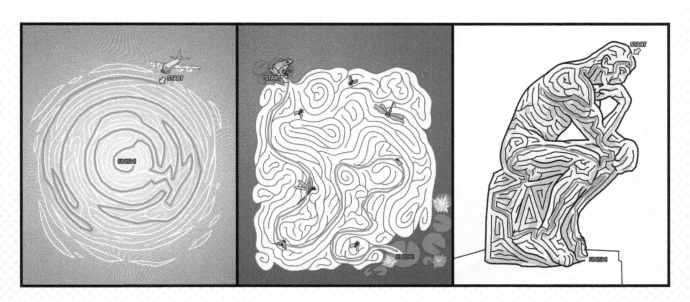

Answers

Page 43:
Cleared for Landing

Page 44:
School's Out

Page 45:
Omnomnom!

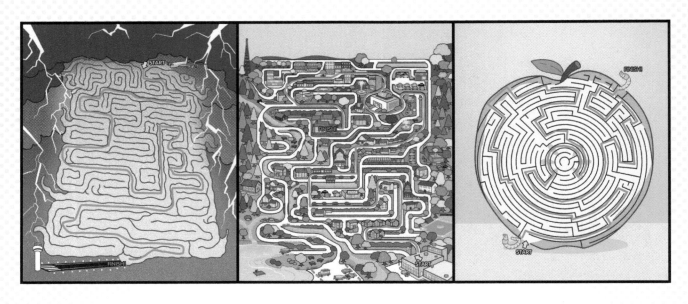

Page 46:
Kick Flip!

Page 47:
The Most Import-*ant* Meal of the Day!

Page 48:
Pangolin Puzzle

Answers ⬇

Page 49:
Tongue-Tied!

Page 50:
Johnny Appleseed

Page 51:
Journey to the Center of the Earth!

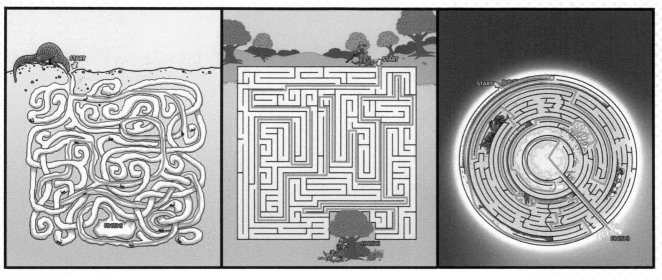

Page 52:
South for the Winter

Page 53:
Modern Art!

Page 54:
Are You My Mummy?

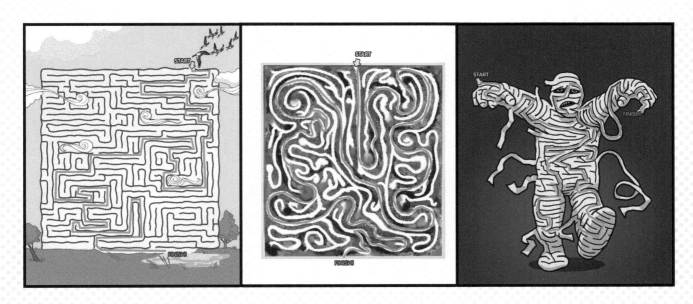

Answers ⬇

Page 55:
Serious Blockage!

Page 56:
Hole-in-One!

Page 57:
Meerkat's Memory

Page 58:
Space Invaders!

Page 59:
Getting Nervous?

Page 60:
Pizza Party!

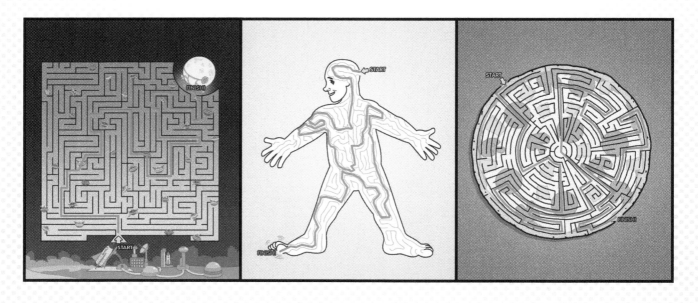

Answers

Page 61:
Time to Hit the Hay!

Page 62:
Movie Night

Page 63:
A-*maze*-ing Graffiti!

Page 64:
Mama Bird

Page 65:
Adventure Time!

Page 66
Sea Monsters!

Answers

Page 67:
Space Walk!

Page 68:
It's Ready to Blow!

Page 69:
Maze-a-saurus Rex!

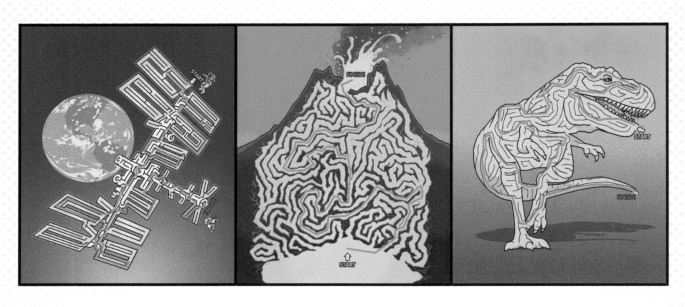

Page 70:
Fun at the Water Park!

Page 71:
Mazes & Monsters

Page 72:
Helicopter Trip

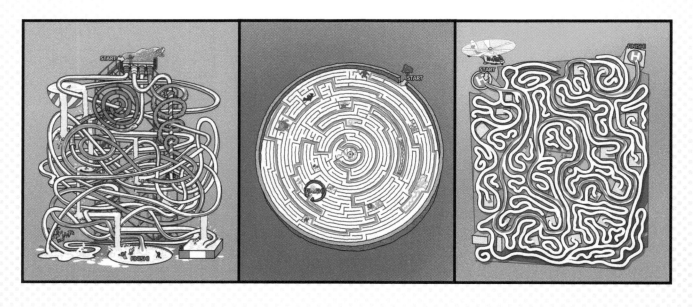

Answers ⬇

Page 73:
Moooooooooove It

Page 74:
The Yellow Brick Road

Page 75:
A Night at the Museum

Page 76:
A Knight to Remember!

Page 77:
Clean. Your. Room!

Page 78:
Reef Races!

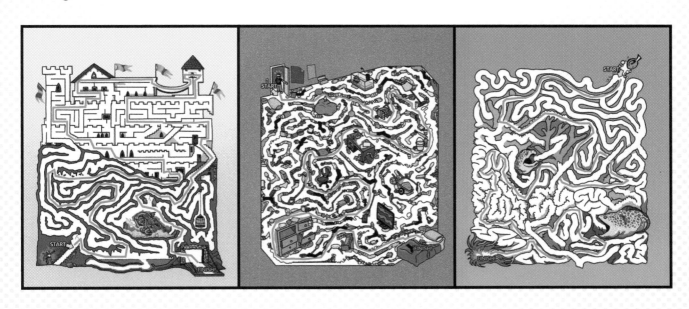

CPSIA information can be obtained
at www.ICGtesting.com
Printed in the USA
LVHW022303010420
651917LV00006B/9

9 781646 118519